SILK paper

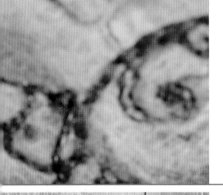
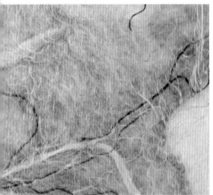

SILK paper

FOR TEXTILE ARTISTS

Sarah Lawrence

A & C Black • London

First published in the UK by
A&C Black Publishers Ltd
38 Soho Square
London W1D 3HB

www.acblack.com

Copyright © 2008 by
Breslich & Foss Ltd

Text by **Sarah Lawrence**
Photographs by **Sussie Bel**l
Design by **Elizabeth Healey**

Conceived and produced by
Breslich & Foss Ltd
2A Union Court
20-22 Union Road
London SW4 6JP

A CIP catalogue record for this book
is available from the British Library.

ISBN: 978-1408-102-688

Printed in China
10 9 8 7 6 5 4 3 2 1

CONTENTS

INTRODUCTION

The Chinese guarded the secret of sericulture, or silkmaking, for many centuries, and so there has always been an air of intrigue, secrecy and romance surrounding silk. Its softness, lustre and its association with luxury and opulence all add to its mystique. My own interest in silk was captured early on in childhood by a box of my mother's beautifully coloured silk threads. They remain to this day in their box—unused because they were silk and deemed too precious to disturb. Happily, over the last twenty years, silk fibres and silk cloth have become less expensive and more readily available, so that silk is no longer the preserve of those with wealth. It has become an affordable medium for textile artists.

I first came across silk fibres and their uses as a felt maker many years ago, and I am grateful to Joan Braganza who organised a weekend of workshops I attended where Inge Evers demonstrated a method of making silk paper. This started me on my journey to develop my own style of working with silk fibres of various types, incorporating them into contemporary textile work.

Above Pieces of silk paper can be further embellished with hand and machine stitches, beading and tassels, as demonstrated here.

I am personally interested in the wider story behind the materials that I use. Just as I like to know where the fibres for my feltmaking come from, I am interested in the historical and ethnographic context of silk fibres as well. I am fascinated by the early history of silk production and how it came to England, by the mistakes and successes made by kings and governments over centuries in order to establish the cultivation of silk; the development of a silk weaving industry, and the way in which the early English settlers in America were encouraged to rear silk worms.

The ability to construct a fabric gives the creative textile artist great freedom to develop a personal style. There is the possibility of total artistic control over the process, from the selection of fibres and the colouring of the silk to the choice of technique, and these are decisions that can dramatically alter the path of creativity.

I like to dye my own silk fibres: I get a real delight from the myriad colours that are created from simple dye processes. I like the variety of textures and types of silk fibre that are available. I like the juxtaposition of lustre, texture and the softness of silk. This is the reason for this book: to give an insight to those who have also been captivated and delighted by the lure of a very thin filament produced by a rather plump caterpillar. I hope that the information contained in this book allows you to develop your own silk style and to get the same amount of enjoyment and artistic satisfaction as I do in creating textile art from silk fibres.

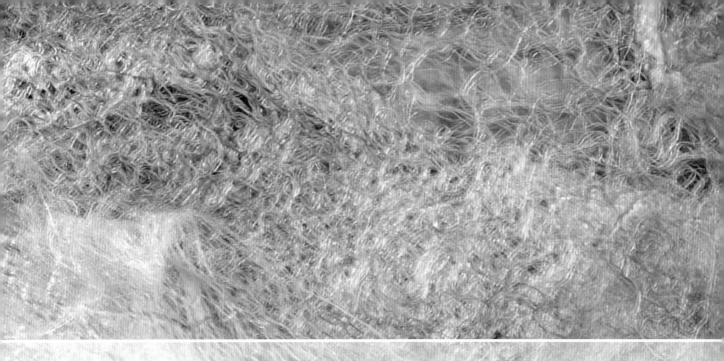

WORKING WITH

SILK

This chapter contains the information you will need about the different types of raw silk from which silk paper can be constructed. There is also information on dyeing silk fibres.

Silk Types

All silk comes from the same source: a cocoon produced by a silk worm. However, many factors affect the type and quality of silk that is produced, not least of which is the species of moth. *Bombyx mori* feeds only on the leaves of the mulberry bush and produces mulberry silk, which is white. Other moth species feed on other plants, which will affect the colour and quality of the silk filament they produce.

Tussah silk is produced by wild silk moths that feed on different foodstuffs and produce a caramel-coloured, very slightly rougher silk fibre. As the silk moth is allowed to emerge from the cocoon, breaking the continuous filament in the process, the cocoons cannot be reeled or 'thrown' as with mulberry silk.

How the cocoons are processed will also affect the quality of the end product which, in the commercial world, is silk thread. There are two principal methods of silk thread production: silk reeling from whole cocoons and manufacture from pierced, cut or damaged cocoons. Fortunately for the creative textile artist, these processes produce by-products and it is these by-products that are used in this book.

THE SILK PRODUCTION PROCESS

Silk reeling is the process by which silk thread is unwound from whole, intact, cocoons that have been softened in hot water. The aim is to draw off filaments that are as long as possible. This gives great strength to the thread that is produced. A number of cocoons are unwound simultaneously with several filaments joined together to form a single thread. As these are still very fine, two or three of these are twined together and reeled onto a skein. This silk filament still retains some gum, hence its name, 'gummy filament.'

One by-product of reeling is the carrier rod, which is made up of silk fibre that builds up on rods over which the silk is drawn. Periodically the rods are cut off to create carrier rod waste. Like cocoons, rods are sold by weight

or by piece by the suppliers listed at the end of the book.

Not all the silk filament in a cocoon can be successfully drawn off as a continuous filament; leftover or broken threads are known as throwster's waste and are another useful by-product for the textile artist. Like rods and cocoons, throwster's waste is gummy, but is often degummed by later processing.

Silk tops and sliver are produced from the remains of the cocoon when as much filament as possible has been extracted. Top is a form of silk in which long fibres are processed into parallel alignment. Top is generally sold by weight in a continuous length, but sometimes it is sold as a 'brick,' a knotted bundle weighing around 150g (5 oz). Silk sliver is a thinner version of top that is usually sold by weight. Noil is a by-product of silk top production, and consists of short, very light fibres. Noil is sold by weight and 30 to 50g (1 to 2 oz) is adequate to begin with.

An alternative production method is used on pierced cocoons (where the moth has emerged) or cut, damaged or double cocoons (where two cocoons have been spun too close together and

Tussah silk

Most commercially produced silk requires the stifling of the pupating moth in order to prevent the damage that the adult moth makes emerging from the cocoon. For those with ethical concerns, tussah silks are an alternative, as the moth emerges before the cocoons are gathered. Which silk to use is a personal, ethical decision and you should research this subject more thoroughly.

bove The silk types shown here are (from
ft to right and top to bottom): silk hankies,
ocoon strippings, raw cocoons, mulberry
lk sliver, gummy throwster's waste,
egummed throwster's waste, tussah silk
iver; silk noil, mawata caps, rods.

ecome inseparable). Because of the
amage, the fibres are shorter in length.
 process these, the cocoons are first
oiled in water to remove the gum
ericin) and make them soft. They are
en turned inside out individually to
emove pupae and other waste. Several
ocoons are stacked and then spread
y hand. These are then hung on a
ame. They are then finished by
ashing and drying. The end result is
lk caps or bells from which spun silk

can be produced. Tops and sliver can
also be produced in this way.

Thus, the way in which cocoons are
handled results in different fibre types
and forms. Some of these forms (such as
the cocoons themselves and carrier
rods), require a degree of preparation
by the textile artist. Other silk types,
such as caps and hankies, can be used
with minimal preparation. The most
useful preparation methods for cocoons,
rods, hankies, and caps are shown on
pages 12 to 21. Later in the book
(pages 110 –123), you'll find projects
that use cocoons and rods in their
unprocessed form.

Sericin

Any silk that has 'gum-in' or 'gummy' in
its name (for example, gummy
throwster's waste) still contains a natural
gum called sericin that binds the silk
fibres to each other in the cocoon.
Sericin is usually removed during the silk
production process. Forms of silk that
contain the gum are cocoon strippings,
carrier rods and, of course, cocoons.
Gummy silk types are used to make silk
using the iron method on page 32.

Silk types that have had the gum
removed are used in the medium
method (page 68) and the stitched
method (page 94). These silk types are
mulberry and tussah tops, sliver,
hankies, and caps. More processed
forms such as condenser waste can
also be used.

Silk cocoons

A silk cocoon is the result of the process undertaken by the silk worm (the larval form of the *Bombyx mori* or silk moth) to create a protective environment while it pupates from a larva to a moth. The process begins when the caterpillar (the silk worm) has reached its maximum size, has eaten as much as it can, and is ready to pupate. It begins to produce a fluid that sets to become a silk filament and is continuous in length. The silk worm needs a vertical support to create the cocoon. In nature this would be a bush but in sericulture (silk production) straw and wood framing is used. The creation of the cocoon takes a couple of days. If the moth is allowed to mature naturally it produces a chemical that dissolves the gum surrounding the silk filament – the sericin – and emerges. However, a broken cocoon is not suitable for reeling so the moth is stifled within the cocoon, which allows for a

Above Here you can see three types of cocoons. (Top) Cut cocoons are usually not the best quality because of their irregular and nobbly shapes. They are sold in their natural state and can be dyed. (Middle) Golden cocoons are very rare, delicate, and lacey. (Bottom) These whole cocoons contain the stifled moth larvae.

Below Stretched cocoons have a wonderful texture that can be put to good use in decorative projects.

continuous filament to be reeled off. Broken or damaged cocoons are generally used for spinning; a spun silk is produced in the same way as a woollen or cotton yarn. Whole cocoons, which tend to be more evenly shaped, are all approximately 5cm (2 in) in size.

A good mulberry silk cocoon can produce more than 400 metres of continuous silk filament. When preparing cocoons it is important to remove the outside layer of silk waste (this is loose fibre). The innermost layer (the envelope), like the skin on a peanut, is also waste. Dupion silk is a spun silk fabric made from double cocoons – irregular shapes that give the fabric its distinctive texture. Silk cocoons can be bought by weight or by piece, and in a natural or undyed state.

The softening and stretching preparation method shown here allows the fibres to be spun out later.

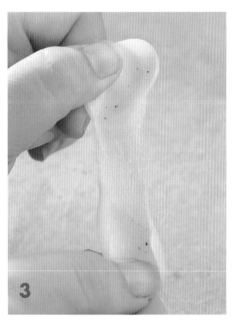

1

Select some whole cocoons and remove any loose waste fibres from their outside to leave the cocoon smooth. (The waste can be used for compost material.) With a sharp pair of scissors, pierce the outer shell and cut through the cocoon to reveal the stifled remains of the silk moth pupa. Discard.

YOU WILL NEED:

• whole cocoons

• small, sharp scissors

• bowl

• tweezers

2 Place the cut and emptied cocoons into a bowl of very hot water and allow them to soak. The cocoons will sink and go translucent when the water has penetrated the fibre layers. This will soften and disrupt the sericin gum surrounding the silk fibres, which will allow them to be stretched and split. You may find that adding a drop of washing-up liquid will assist in the soaking process.

3 Use tweezers to remove the softened cocoons from the bowl, as they may still be hot. Use pliers to begin pulling the cocoon apart; as the material cools, you will be able to use your fingers. The cocoon can be stretched to create a very distinctive sheet. After a while it will become difficult to pull and stretch the silk because the sericin that was softened by the hot water will begin to set again. At this point you can repeat the softening process described in Step 2.

4 Continue to stretch the cocoon to create a textured fabric that can be utilised in many projects.

Rods

Carrier rod waste is formed over a metal rod in the reeling process. The rods themselves are stick-like in shape and generally about 15cm (6 in) long. As the silk waste builds up on the rod during the silk production process, it is sliced away to keep the rod clean. The resulting waste is very hard and laden with sericin. The rods themselves can be used as structural items just as they are, or they can be cut and dyed. In this example I used dyed rods. A useful way to incorporate rods into textile pieces is to separate the layers into thin sheets of silk fibre. Carrier rod waste can be bought by weight or by piece, and in a natural or undyed state.

1   Take a dyed or natural coloured rod and open up the structure.

2   Bend the strip of silk back onto its spine and begin to curl the end back on itself.

3   Continue to curl the rod until a tight roll is formed.

YOU WILL NEED:

• rods in a natural or dyed state

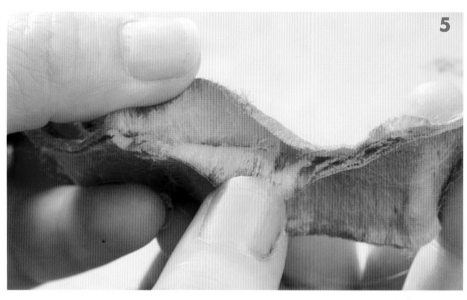

4 Roll this silk mass between your hands several times until the fibres soften. The continuous movement and pressure from your hands will break the rigid structure created by the sericin gum.

5 Open out the softened silk ribbon. You will notice that the edge has begun to separate into layers.

6 Carefully peel away each layer.

7 Some of the layers that you have separated will be complete; others will be short or broken. This really does not matter, as these pieces can be used as they are.

Creating threads

1   To produce a thread, stretch out a single delaminated ribbon of silk.

2   You will notice that, as the ribbon of fibre is stretched out, a very distinctive lattice pattern emerges. These pieces can be used for decorative projects just as they are.

3   Take one end of the stretched silk ribbon and twist it to create a very decorative slubbed yarn.

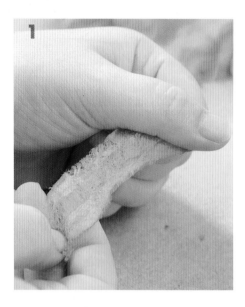

TIP

A slubbed yarn, such as the thread made here, is an irregular or uneven yarn. Slubbed yarns can be used for decorative knitting or stitching.

Top Carrier rod waste in its undyed form.

Above Twisted carrier rod yarn ready for use in a project.

Right Thin layers taken from rose-coloured rods can be rolled up to form silk roses.

Silk hankies

Silk hankies are flat, stretched cocoons that are roughly square in shape and about 20 x 20cm (8 x 8 in): the size of a Victorian lady's handkerchief. Hankies are supplied in multilayered stacks because they are made from many cocoons. In one corner of the stack of layers there is a hole that marks the place where the edge of the softened cocoons was placed to allow purchase for the stretching process.

To utilise this silk form, look carefully at the edge of a stack of hankies and you will notice that each layer is reasonably identifiable. If you pull the dry layers apart slowly, they will be difficult to separate as the fibres cling together between the layers. Pull apart in one swift motion. When dyeing hankies, I like to separate them at the end of the process before they dry out because wet hankies are easier to separate.

Hankies can be used as they are to create silk paper, but they can also be used to create a yarn. Traditionally hankies are placed onto specialised spinning equipment and the fibres spun out. I have not yet fully mastered the art of spinning so the yarns that I create are textural rather than technically correct. I would advise anyone who is interested in developing this method to draw on the experience of friends who are more accomplished in the art of spinning. It is relatively easy to set this up for drop spindling. Further ways use silk hankies are described throughout the book.

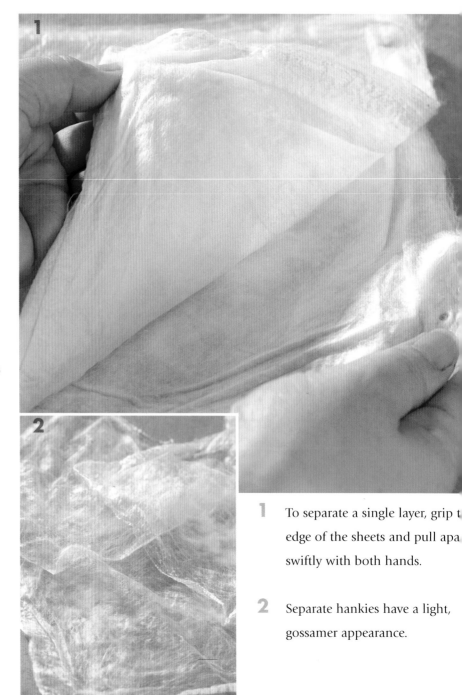

1 To separate a single layer, grip the edge of the sheets and pull apart swiftly with both hands.

2 Separate hankies have a light, gossamer appearance.

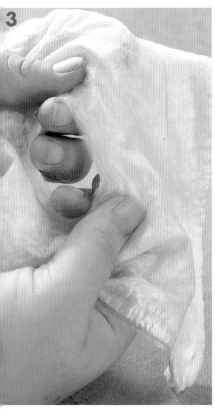

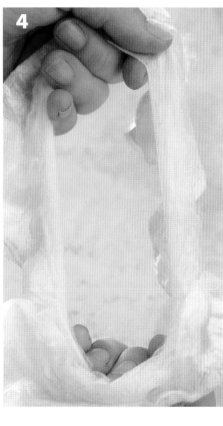

3 Grasp a hankie in both hands and rip a hole in the centre.

4 Begin to pull apart the hankie.

5 Break off a section of hankie from the inner ring.

6 Begin to twist the yarn into a thread. To prevent it becoming knotted up, you may wish to roll the thread around a straw.

7 Form the thread into a ball ready for a project (knitting).

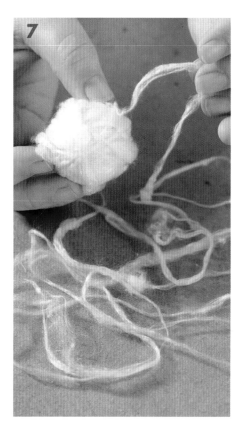

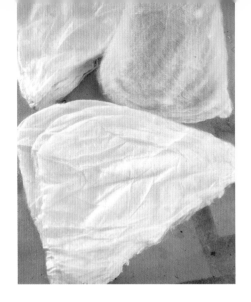

Mawata caps

Mawata caps have a bell-like shape that is formed by workers opening out and stretching cocoons over a domed former. To prepare a silk yarn from stretched caps, you will need the assistance of another person.

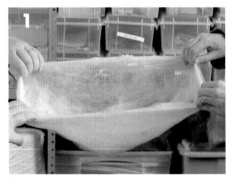

1 Take the edge of the cap and stretch it into a square, making sure your partner has a firm grasp of the other end.

2 With one partner holding firmly onto the edge, the other partner should pull the cap toward themselves. The cap will be quite resistant, but eventually you will feel the silk fibres loosen and give way under pressure.

3 Both partners can now begin to stretch out the sheet of silk.

4 Continue to stretch out a rectangular shape, holding firmly onto the edges.

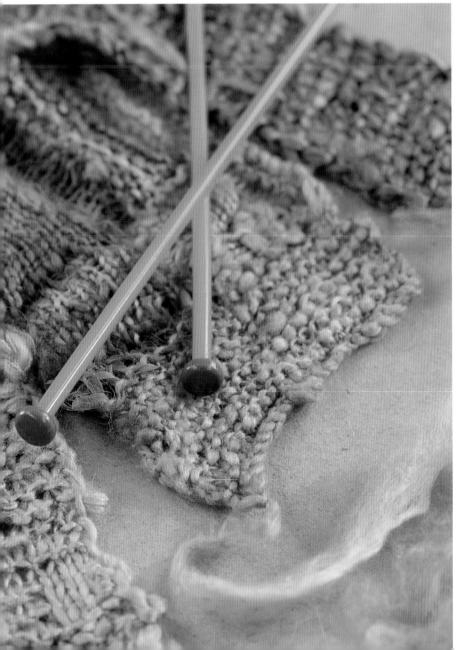

5 Eventually you will create a very fine cobweb. This can then be elongated and stretched to form a continuous rope of silk.

6 Twist gently to make a new silk thread that can be used for knitting or hand stitch work. If you are able to use a drop spindle or a spinning wheel, you will create a finer more consistent thread. Wind the newly created silk thread into a ball ready for use. You can do this by hand or use a mechanical ball winder. In my experience it is not necessary to ply two threads together for this very basic yarn. However, if you are able to find out more about conventional spinning and yarn making this will definitely improve your ability to make a consistent or creative yarn. With patience, enough yarn can be spun to produce a small knitted garment.

Left Samples of knitting made from stretched, dyed mawata caps. These were knitted on medium sized needles (chosen because they were pretty!). The knitted fabric has a pleasing slubbed or uneven surface. Knitted pieces like these can be incorporated into silk fabric using the iron method. (See pages 44 to 45.)

Dyeing

Although the tone and texture of silk in its natural state is beautiful, you can also create a medley of colours by dyeing the silk. The lustre and luminosity of dyed silk fibres are truly wonderful. The simple but effective dyeing methods described in the following pages will allow you to create your own colour palette for the projects you have in mind. The way fibres are laid down in the various dyeing methods ensures that the different colours in the fibres will mingle in any silk that you dye, even when the fibres are layered on top of each other (unless the layers are very dense). The following methods of dyeing allow you to create a bold, bright, powerful palette should you wish, or an elegantly subtle display. Remember, even when you have dyed your chosen silk fibres, if you are not completely satisfied with the colour blends, then you can just over-dye them (repeat the dyeing process) to create new colour blends.

It is always helpful to have a selection of dyed caps and hankies stored and ready for use in projects.

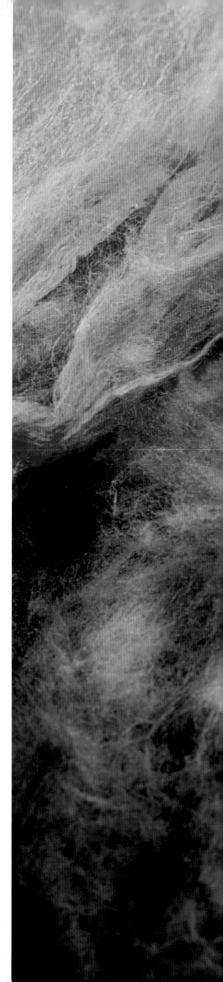

Types of dye

There are various dyes available which are easy to use and need a minimum of equipment. The dyes I have used in this chapter are easily available, simple to use, and give very good results. Whether using acid or procion dyes, or the all-in-one liquid dyes that require steam or heat from a microwave, remember that you can mix colours within dye types to suit your particular project.

Acid dyes

Acid dyes are used to colour wool and other animal or protein fibres. Fibres such as silk and synthetics (nylon) are also dyed with these dyes. Acidic conditions are required to fix acid dyes. These are generally achieved by adding white vinegar or, in some cases ammonium sulphate crystals, to water.

GUIDELINES FOR DYE-TO-FIBRE WEIGHT

DRY WEIGHT TO BE DYED	VINEGAR	WATER
50g (1¾ oz)	50ml (1¾ fl oz)	1.5 l (6⅓ cups)
100g (3½ oz)	100ml (3½ fl oz)	3 l (12⅔ cups)
200g (7 oz)	200ml (7 fl oz)	6 l (25⅓ cups)

The above are only guidelines. As you gain experience in dyeing, you will find that you may use less dye, as the saturation of these dyes is strong.

MAKING UP DYE STOCK

Feel free to alter the values of this basic recipe to suit the colour strength needed for your projects.

YOU WILL NEED:
- clean containers (large drinking cups or similar or screw top jars)
- assorted acid dyes
- measuring spoons
- measuring cup
- wooden coffee stirrers

Measure 300 ml (1¼ cups) of liquid and add 63 ml (⅛ tsp) of acid dye powder. Mix with a wooden coffee stirrer or similar. It is important that each colour has its own set of stirrers to avoid cross contamination of colour. If not used all at once, this dye stock can be kept in an airtight/screw top jar for several months. Should the liquid evaporate, it can be revived with the addition of water. Note that these liquid to powder ratios are approximate, and you may want to adjust the colour strength by adding a bit more, or a bit less, powder.

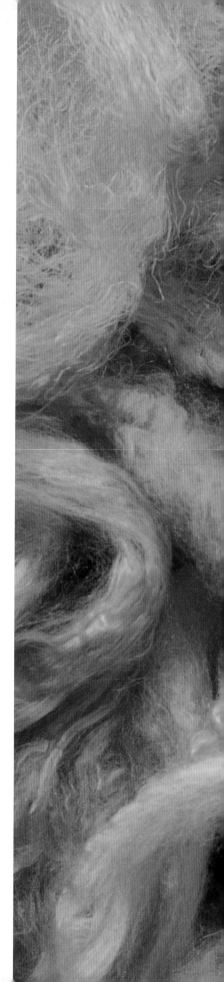

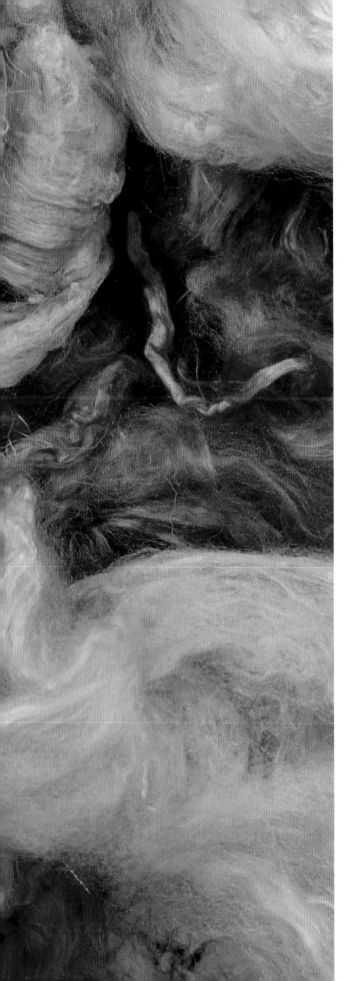

Procion dyeing

Silk fibre and, indeed, other silk materials are unusual in that they can be dyed with acid dyes and procion dyes. Acid dyes are usually intended for animal protein materials, such as wool. Procion dyes are generally recognised as being suitable for plant materials or cellulose-based materials. I have not used procion dyeing in this book because it requires a more considered approach than acid dyeing. Generally, I would recommend that procion is best used by people who wish to dye large volumes of silk.

Procion dyes will only work when there is a high alkaline presence. This is why soda crystals are dissolved in water and added to the dye bath. This makes the dye reactive, and the salt solution encourages the dye to leave the water and interact with the materials being dyed. Always follow the manufacturer's instructions when using procion dyes.

Rainbow dyeing

Before applying the dye, the silk must be prepared to accept it. To do this, place your chosen silk sliver in a large bowl containing a small amount of white vinegar to acidify the water. The acid in the vinegar will help to bind the dye to the silk fibres. Although there are lots of very precise recipes, I find that in a bowl containing approximately 3 litres (5 pints) of water, half a cup of white vinegar is sufficient. (Don't use darker malted vinegar as this is too pungent.) Leave the fibres to soak overnight or until they slightly swell and turn translucent. Check that there are no dry patches, as dry areas will not dye. Take your fibres out of the water and firmly wring them out. Don't be afraid to squeeze: silk fibres are incredibly

strong and you will see that the sliver rope remains intact.

If you choose to use mulberry silk sliver, the whiter fibres will offer a purer colour; if tussah sliver is used, the darker fibres will enrich the colour that is added to it.

1 On a suitable work surface, stretch out two layers of cling film approximately 60cm (2 ft) in length. Take the wetted fibres and lay them out in lines, leaving about 15cm (6 in) clear at either end of the plastic wrap.

2 Taking your dye pots and sponge brush, sponge lines of dye across the width of the silk slivers by repeatedly dabbing and reloading the sponge brush with dye mix. This will create very clear areas of colour.

3 Continue to add lines of dye in a second colour, using a new foam brush per dye pot. By adding blue, the red dye already applied will develop a purple line where the two colours meet.

YOU WILL NEED:

- cling film
- 50 g (1¾ oz) or more of silk sliver
   acid dyes
- foam brushes
- large bowl
- vinegar
- microwave
- latex or rubber gloves
- plate

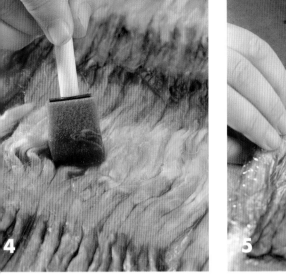

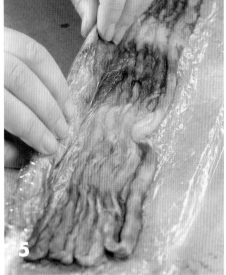

ght Rainbow-dyed
k sliver that has
een left to dry
doors.

4 When yellow is added, it will create green when it meets the blue dye and orange where it runs into the red. If you find the colour is not as intense as you expected, add a few more grains of acid dye to the dye pots to make a stronger solution. Apply repeatedly to the sliver until you are happy with the colour.

5 Very carefully roll up the plastic wrap like a Swiss roll.

6 Roll into a spiral and put it onto a microwave-proof dish. Place in a microwave oven and cook on the highest setting for two to three minutes. If you don't have a microwave, place the roll in a steamer and steam for half an hour. It is the heat-activated reaction between the dye, silk, and acid that fixes the colour onto the surface of the silk.

7 Carefully remove the heated fibres from the microwave and open out the roll. Allow to cool. When cool, rinse the newly dyed fibres in warm water so that excess unwanted dye stock is removed. Rinse until the water is clear, then allow the fibres to dry.

Microwave random dyeing

There are a number of liquid products available for dyeing silk. Most of these products contain both colour and fixative and can be applied directly to wetted silk fibres. Please read individual manufacturer's instructions, as processing may vary slightly. These easily applied, all-in-one dyes are available in many colours and, like most other dye stuffs, can be mixed or blended to create unique colour combinations.

Before dyeing, prepare the silk fibres by soaking them in warm water. You can also add a drop of washing-up liquid to accelerate the wetting process. When the fibres are thoroughly soaked, wring them out and place them in a shallow plastic container. In this project, I've used (top to bottom) sliver, condenser waste and noil.

YOU WILL NEED:

- a selection of liquid colour dyes
- a selection of silk fibres such as noil, condenser waste and silk sliver
- shallow plastic container
- latex or rubber gloves

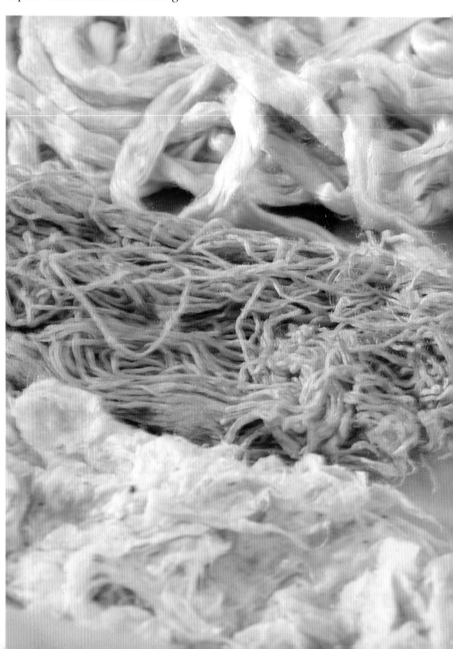

Squirt the first colour randomly over the fibres.

Add the second and third colours, adjust the first if necessary. By using yellow, blue and red, a myriad of colours will be achieved.

Squeeze up the fibres, keeping them in separate heaps.

Place in a microwave oven and cook on the highest setting for two to three minutes. After the colour has been activated, the fibres should be rinsed until no excess colour remains and the water runs clear. Allow the fibres to dry out before using them in a project.

PROJECTS
THE

THE IRON METHOD

This method is quick and simple and uses different kinds of 'gummy' silk. Sericin is generally removed in the industrial process, but gummy silk is a type of fibre that has not had the outer sericin removed. The addition of moisture and the play of heat over the surface of the silk fibres reinvigorates the sericin and softens it enough for it to bind the fibres to each other. When the paper is cool and has dried, the sericin reverts to its natural state and has the effect of gluing the fibres to each other. The result is a strong paper that you can cut up or decorate further.

The types of gummy silk suitable for this method are cocoon strippings in a natural and a yellow form, gummy throwster's waste and gummy filament. (See the Glossary on page 126 for a fuller explanation of these terms.) Silk fibres can be used alone or in combination with others. Used on its own, a fibre will have a distinct 'personality' of texture and function: smooth, random, and chaotic or a distinct pattern. Using fibres in combination (for example, gummy throwster's waste with filament) will allow you to produce endless textural variations.

Before laying out the fibres, arrange your work area, which should be a heat-resistant surface. Cut some newspaper or plain newsprint slightly larger than the work surface. The newspaper absorbs the excess moisture that is created when the iron is used on the arrangement of fibres, and it protects any surrounding work space from the colour spray application. Lay a sheet of silicon or baking parchment on top of the newspaper.

THE IRON METHOD

YOU WILL NEED:

- newspaper or newsprint
- heat resistance surface
- a roll or several sheets of non-stick baking parchment or similar
- approximately 10g (½ oz) of gum-in fibres, such as cocoon strippings, gummy throwster's waste or gummy filament
- spritzer bottle
- iron – either a travel sized one or an ordinary one

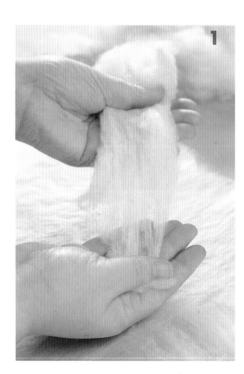

Lay out the cocoon strippings on the baking parchment. To do this, hold the bulk fibre in one hand and pull out small handfuls. The fibres are usually well aligned and can be pulled away in small drifts.

Lay out the fibres so they overlap each other on the sheet of baking parchment. You can lay them in neat rows (as shown here) or more randomly. If you want to end up with an evenly gauged silk paper then you will need to 'tweak' the layers so they appear even.

To make a natural coloured paper, simply spray cold water in a light mist over the fibres. Hold the spritzer about 20cm (8 in) above the surface of the fibres.

Place another piece of baking parchment on top of the pile of fibres.

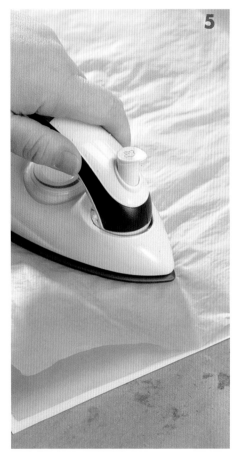

5 Iron over the surface of the baking parchment with a medium to hot iron. (Do not use the steam setting.) You may hear a 'sizzle' as the water mist is heated by the iron. This is normal! Iron methodically over the surface for a few seconds.

6 You can unpeel the baking parchment and the silk paper at this stage, which will be a little limp, and set it aside to dry and harden up.

TIP

The way in which you lay out the fibres will have an effect on how the finished paper looks. In this project, the fibres are laid out in regular lines. To create the effect of contrasting denser and thinner areas (where the fibres are fine enough to see through), lay the fibres out randomly instead. The more experience you have of pulling the fibres the more you will gain confidence in arranging them for the project you have in mind.

7 The back of the paper (shown here) is softer than the front.

8 If you don't want the delicate wispy edges that naturally occur, the edges can be folded over and ironed. If the silk paper is a little dry, lightly re-spritz where the fold will be. Fold the baking parchment over and iron along the crease. If you iron directly onto the newly formed silk paper, the iron will stick to it and spoil your work.

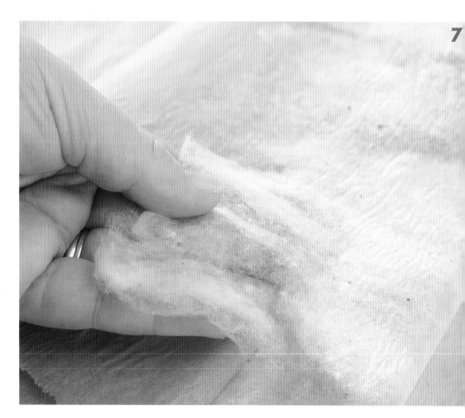

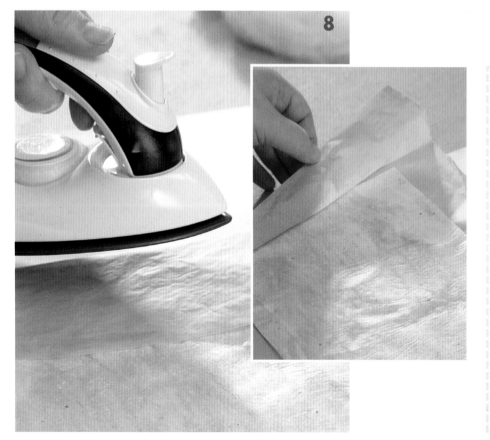

TIP

To create a stronger paper (suitable 3-D constructed pieces and projects that are going to have shapes cut or punched out of them or be stitched), flip the 'sandwich' over in Step 6, p the parchment from the back and sp the fibres lightly again with water. Replace the parchment and re-iron for a few seconds.

Adding embellishments

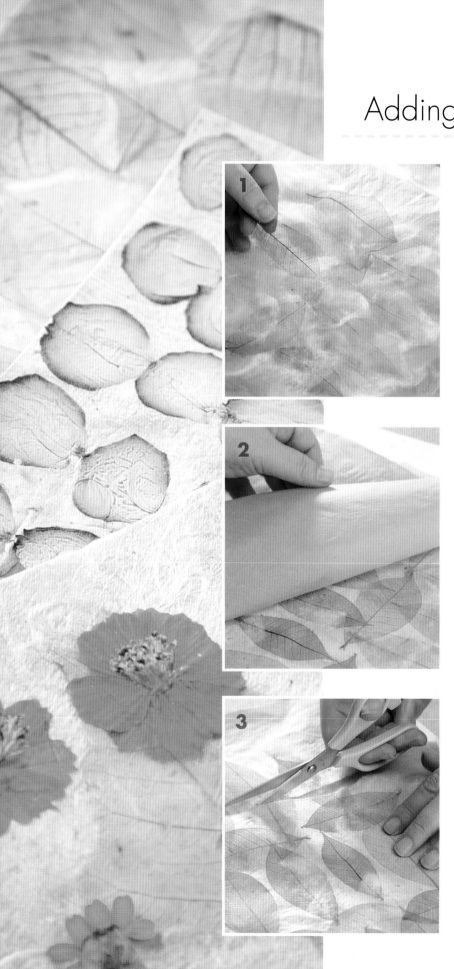

I like to add lightweight natural additions to my papers, such as rose petals, dried flowers, leaves, autumnal seed cases and sinamays (woven material made from banana fibres). These complement the style of the silk paper that the iron method creates.

1   Lay the natural things on the spritzed fibres in Step 3, cover with a few more fibres and spritz.

2   Cover with baking parchment and iron as you did in Steps 4 and 5. The sericin that the heat and moisture reactivates draws in these additions and 'glues' them to the fibres.

3   Instead of folding over the edges and ironing, you can also trim the piece to size with scissors.

Adding colour

A simple and effective way to colour the fibres is to use spray colours instead of water. Although you can dye your own fibres beforehand using the microwave method or another method of your choice (see Dyeing, page 22), I have found this method of colouring to be fast, effective and fun to do.

1   Spray on a combination of colourants directly (as shown) or through a stencil. Place the baking parchment on top and iron.

2   If you want to add gold or metal flakes, sprinkle them on the fibres before ironing.

A coloured paper with metallic highlights makes a lovely piece in itself, or can be further embellished or used in other projects.

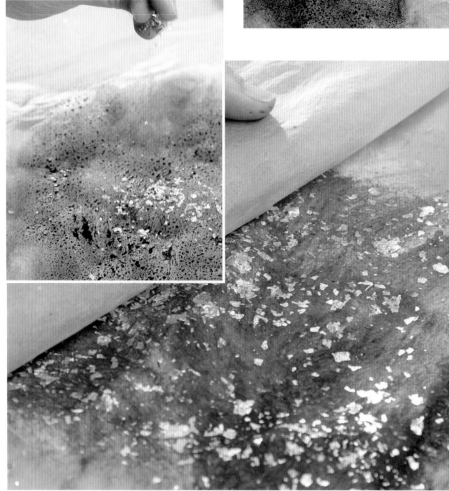

To enrich the colour, flip the sandwich over and spritz a different colour onto the back of the fibres. Replace the parchment and iron.

Flip over the sandwich and peel back the baking parchment to reveal the colour of the reverse side. Fold in the edges and carefully iron over the baking parchment.

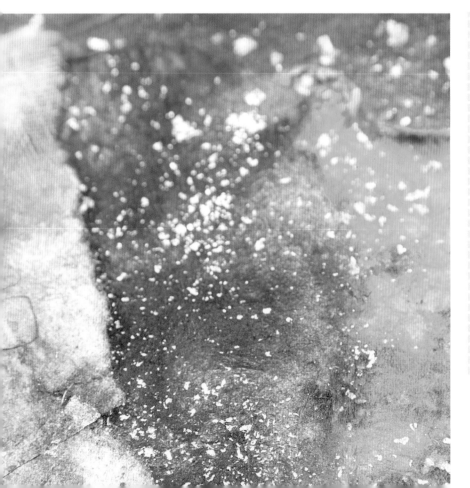

Layering with sinamay

Natural products – such as sinamay – can be included in silk paper with the iron method. Sinamay is made from banana fibres and has a very open weave. It is used widely in hat-making. To integrate sinamay into a piece of silk paper, lay it over the unprocessed fibres and spray it with colour or plain water, then iron as normal. The sinamay will be held in place by the gummy sericin in the silk fibres. The inlaid structure is ideal for further decoration and lends support to the construction of boxes and containers. A simple box can be created by folding, cutting and assembling. The simplest way to make a pattern is by undoing and drawing around a paper carrier bag.

Above In this sample, thin strips of silk paper were cut and interwoven over the sinamay surface. Then the piece was decorated with hand stitches as well as mother-of-pearl discs and beads.

Left To create this piece, I inserted a small section of openly woven sinamay between layers of cocoon strippings. The piece was then lightly coloured with bronze and mauve sprays. When dry, I added small gold squares, painted in acrylic. Finally, I stitched separate backed squares of copper-coloured silk paper onto the surface. The backing lifts the squares away from the flat surface of the silk both physically and visually. I then created free motion blocks around the golden squares. The pattern was then further embellished with copper-coloured square sequins and multicoloured bronze and blue iridescent beads.

bove This container was made from a ombination of silk filament and cocoon rippings, using the iron method. The simple ox construction has a turn over top to show e contrast between the web-like surface of e outside (made by the silk filaments) and e smoother surface inside. Extra decoration as added with woven strips of silk paper ith decorated with mother-of-pearl button nd beads.

Right One piece of iron method silk paper with open-meshed sinamay incorporated into it was used to form this container, which was then embellished with simple hand stitches and mother-of-pearl buttons and beads. This piece is not lined, but a simple cloth lining could easily be made for it.

oposite These silk flowers were
ide using the iron method, cut
t with a template (see page
?4) and folded into shape. The
ckground is iron method silk
per to which sinamay has
en added.

n this sample, a
piece of silk
paper was
made with a
layer of
sinamay. The
paper was then
embellished with
bold hand
stitches to create
texture.

ADDING KNITTING

Create dynamic surfaces by laying knitted pieces onto gummy silk then ironing them as normal. Spray colour will easily be taken up by natural fibres such as cotton, linen and silk. This will result in an integrated and harmonious texture. Further enhancements can be made to the surface with hand or machine stitching, although the new fabric may need to be stabilised with a backing to prevent the different thicknesses of the surface from puckering when the machine stitch is applied. If knitting is not your strongest craft skill, don't worry; so long as the stitches are somehow connected, dropped stitches will add to the drama of the surface. Any loose stitches will be secured by the fusion of the silk to the natural knitted surface. If you can only purl and knit, use very large needles to create the open structure that is best suited for incorporation into a silk surface.

Right The interest in this piece is created by the contrast of strong texture with natural tones as the knit structure meets the smooth addition of silk fibres.

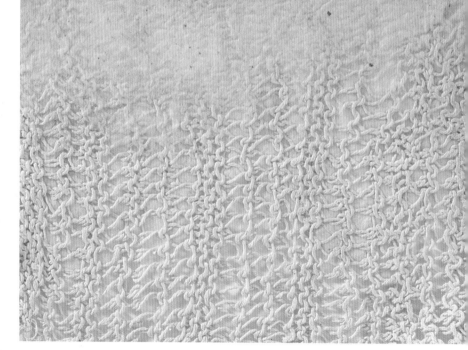

ove The knit structure in this piece uses a
mbination of knit and purl stitches only,
eating texture and contrast that then
eracts with the smoothness of the silk.
me fancy yarns were used, but the
ajority are cotton and silk.

ght The knitted element in this sample was
eated from dyed, spun mawata hankies
e page 18). The silk paper background
as further enhanced with simple stitches to
ild up more texture and to create a
aduated effect between the knitting and
e silk paper.

Heat embossing

Embossing with thermo-reactive powder is a lovely way to add a discrete motif to the surface of a piece of silk paper. There are many powders from which to choose: fine grade powders create a smooth, low-relief effect. Larger crystals result in a more raised finish and a slightly 'distressed' look, which adds character to a piece.

1 Tap the embossing ink onto the rubber stamp to get an even coverage. Stamp the image onto the silk.

2 Sprinkle the printed area with the embossing powder.

YOU WILL NEED:

- heat-resistant surface
- embossing ink
- rubber stamp with an open design, found objects, corks or home-made printing blocks
- sheet of dry silk paper made using the iron method
- embossing powder or crystals
- copy paper
- heat gun

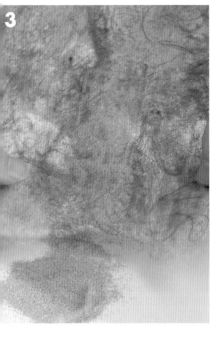

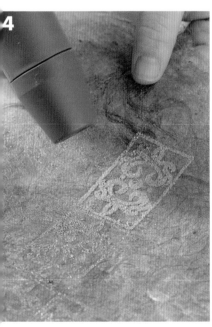

3 Tip the excess powder onto a piece of copy paper and replace it in its original container. Repeat Steps 1 to 3 until the embossed design is completed.

4 Activate the embossing powder or crystals with the heat gun. Don't concentrate the heat on one area, instead distribute the heat evenly until all the granules have melted.

5 You will notice that the granules melt and change under the heat.

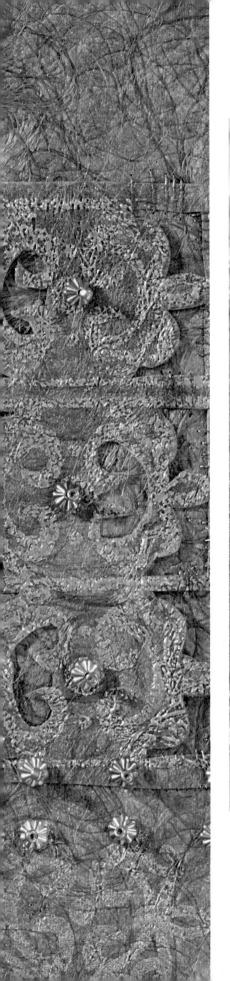

Left A section of embossing has been cut to create an open design, which is then laid onto a silk background that is also embossed. A simple running stitch attaches both pieces together, and it is completed with the addition of small beads.

Above This shows a repeated image printed onto silk paper and then dusted with gold embossing powder.

Moulding

The rubber stamp or sheet you use in this process should be very clean, as any colour on it may transfer to the silk. After a couple of uses, you will find that the rubber will be a little sticky because of the sericin that is released from the gummy silk fibres.

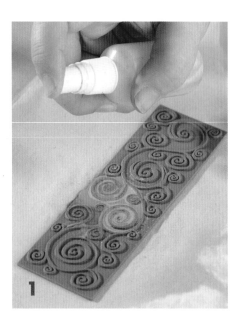

1 Place a sheet of silicone paper on the work surface, then spray the surface of the rubber stamp with water or colour spray. The liquid helps to create the moulded silk and also acts as a release agent.

2 Place generous amounts of loose silk fibre onto the mould and spray on more colour.

3 Spray colour generously over the top of the fibre pile.

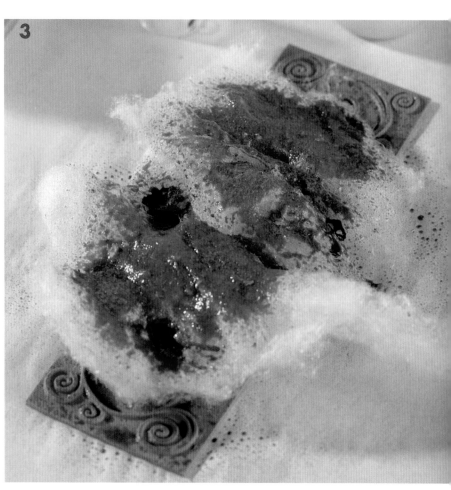

YOU WILL NEED:

- heat-resistant surface
- 2 sheets of silicone paper
- rubber stamp or moulding sheet with an open or deeply etched design
- colour spray of your choice or water spray
- cocoon strippings
- iron

Place the second silicone sheet over the fibres and, using a hot setting, iron the layers. As soon as you see the shadow of the mould appear, stop ironing.

Quickly, in one swift motion, turn the mould over and remove the cast silk away from the mould. It is always best to remove the cast silk from the mould immediately, although please note that it may be quite warm to handle. However, if you leave it to cool, the sericin will harden, making it difficult to remove the cast effectively. Because a lot of liquid is used to colour the silk, it can take a while to dry out. When the casts are dry they can be stitched, glued and cut. The cast silk can also be enhanced by over-painting or patinating the surface with shoe polish or gilding waxes.

Above A collection of silk casts, waiting to be used in decorative projects.

Above This small moulded panel has been overstitched and bound with machine stitching.

Right This textile panel incorporates cast silk motifs, beads, machine stitchery and mother-of-pearl shapes. Some cast elements were cut away and used as single decorative motifs. Cast elements like these can be used to make small pieces of jewellery, such as brooches: simply cut to shape, line the back and attach an appropriate fastener.

Using dimensional paste

Adding a touch of luxury to the surface of silk papers with dimensional paste is simple to do and the results are elegant. Dimensional paste is a thick, viscose, gel-like material that is available in many types and colours. Other materials – such as fine glitter, accent beads and gilding flakes – can be mixed into the paste before it is applied to add further interest.

1 Lay the stencil over the silk paper base. Tape around the edges of the stencil with low-tack tape to secure the stencil and protect the edges.

2 Carefully remove the dimensional paste from the tube with a palette knife. Drag the paste over the stencil. Keep the palette knife at a low angle so that the paste is delivered evenly.

YOU WILL NEED:

- stencil, brass or plastic (the deeper the stencil the more raised the result will be)
- piece of silk paper
- low-tack tape
- dimensional paste
- palette knife or a piece of stiff plastic

3

Below Because I used gummy throwster's waste for this sample, the resulting stencil is slightly 'fuzzy' rather than crisp and clean.

When the area of the stencil is filled, remove the tape and lift the stencil away with a confident movement. If you hesitate you may smudge the image. Remove the stencil before the paste dries or it will stick to the fibres. If you don't intend to reuse it immediately, wash the stencil with warm soapy water and leave to dry. Once dry, the piece can be over-coloured with patinating waxes, acrylic paints and crafters' chalks or embroidered.

Above The piece was coloured using olive and pink tones, then overstitched with a pre-programmed pattern using pale green and pink variegated thread. Blocks and layers were assembled by cutting and layering the decorated silk surface, then embellished with small metal rings (heishi beads) and pale yellow seed beads.

In this sample I made use of a dragonfly stencil and gold tone dimensional paste.

Die-cutting

Interesting and intricate patterns can be made on the surface of silk papers with various shaped punching tools. If the front and back of a single sheet of silk paper are different colours, folding back a flap will create a colourful contrast on the surface.

1   Using a half circle die and a hammer, mark out a gently curving line.

2   Fold up the cut flaps. This allows for many decorative possibilities.

YOU WILL NEED:

- self-heal cutting mat
- selection of dies (sharp punching tools)
- 2 pieces of silk paper in contrasting colours
- craft hammer
- small container

3   Cut further spaces using the slo[t]
    and ribbon dies. The small piec[es]
    that are removed in the die-
    cutting process can be kept in a
    small pot and used as decorativ[e]
    elements in other projects.

4   Cut away a large border from th[e]
    die-cut edge. Shape these edges
    using a half-moon cutter to for[m]
    an arched or staggered wave
    effect. Choose a background
    paper in a contrasting colour.

5   Thread a small ribbon of silk
    paper in and out of the slots
    created.

Opposite Arrange the die-cut sections on
background paper chosen in Step 4. Place
them so that the spaces and openings
created with the die-cutting tools are show[n]
to best effect: make sure there is a strong
colour where they appear. I developed this
piece further with beads and hand stitchin[g.]
The green elements on the finished item are
Victorian foiled glass discs.

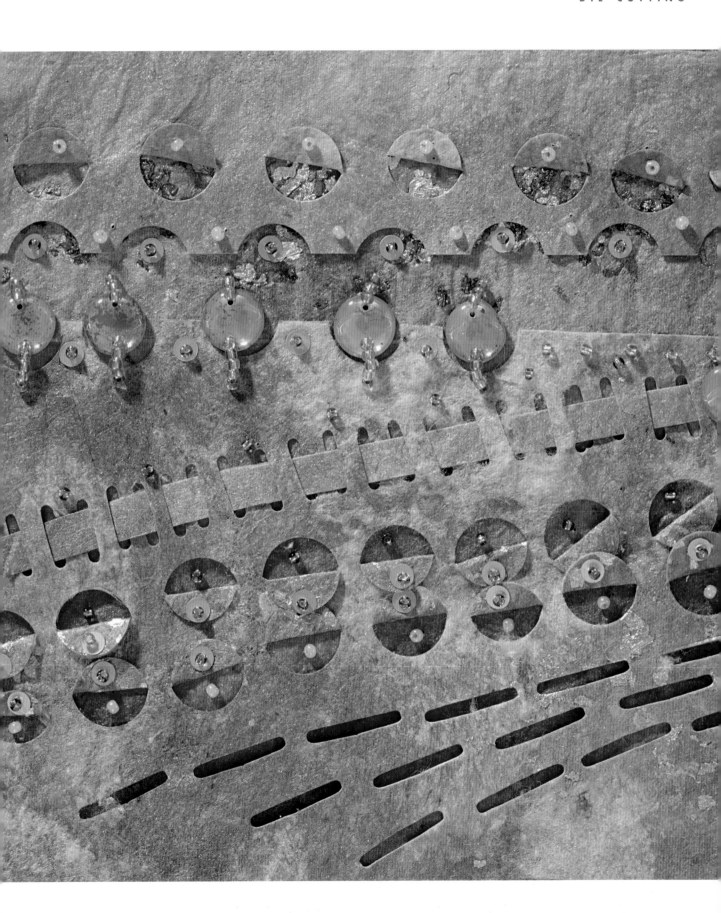

Simple slots laced with a contrasting strip of silk paper creates a wonderful detail for a book page or greeting card.

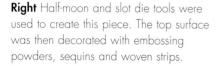

Right Half-moon and slot die tools were used to create this piece. The top surface was then decorated with embossing powders, sequins and woven strips.

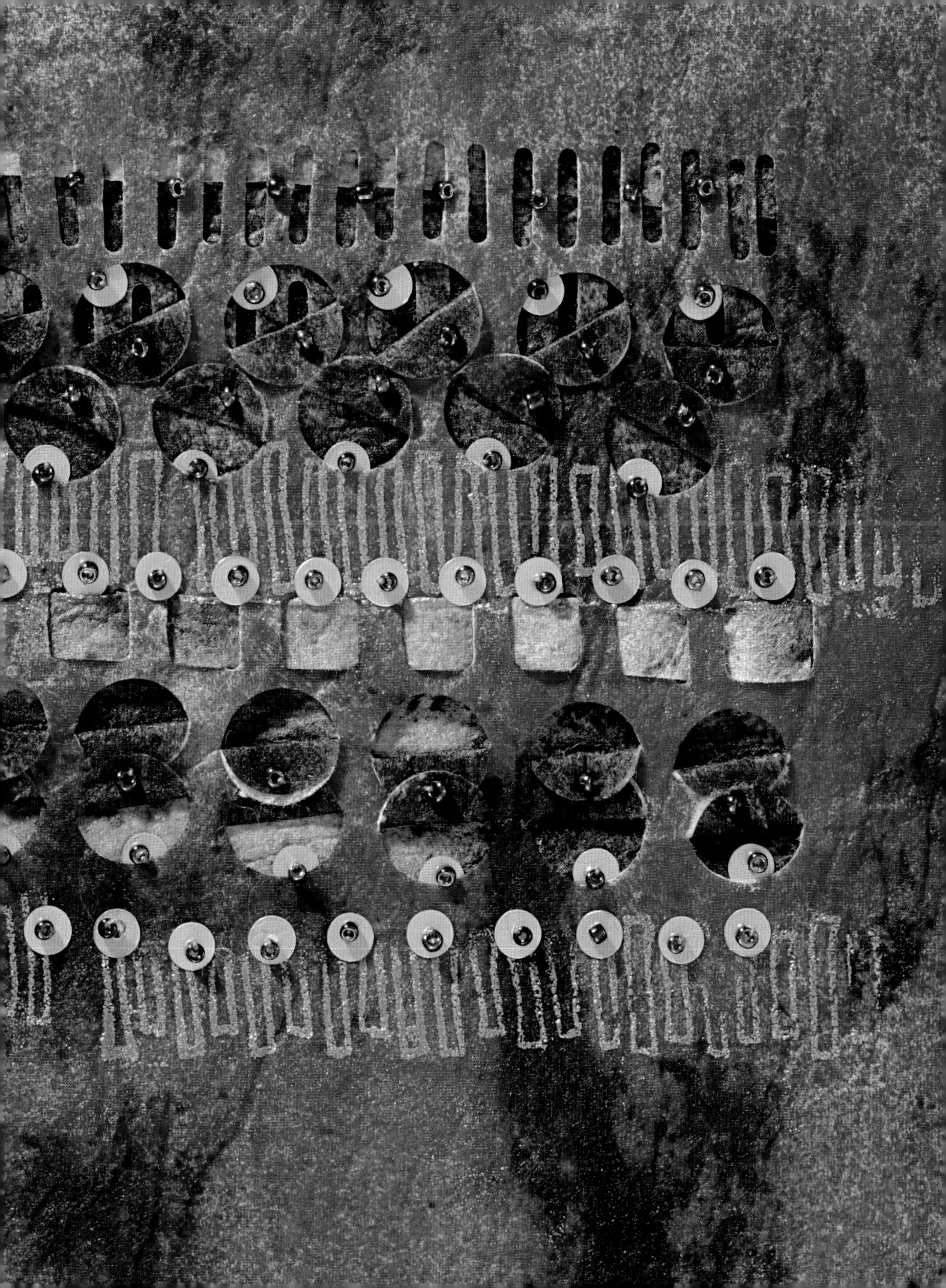

LACÉ WORK

Sheets of silk paper made using the iron method are best for this decorative process, because the paper is crisp and easy to cut. The technique is probably Dutch in origin, but the word lacé is French and means laced or linked together. Use a sheet that is a different colour or tone on each side and remember that you can add light decorative elements, such as metal flake or threads, should you wish. (See page 39.) There are many metal templates for this decorative process, but it is far more fun to cut and fold back shapes that you have created yourself. For this you will need a sharp, fine-bladed craft knife or fine pointed scissors, a ruler and a pencil.

Cut designs through the silk paper. Once all the slots or slits have been cut, the pattern pieces can be folded back. Lightly scoring the folds will help to create a much neater fold. The folded pieces can be layered over each other or simply interlocked. When you have cut and folded your pieces, you can decorate the multicoloured and multilayered surface further with long hand stitches. If you are using a heavy thread, you may need to use a steel point (stiletto) or large gauged bodkin to make a pilot hole through the silk paper layers for the thread to pass through easily. Adding bugle beads of different

lengths can enhance the geometric quality of the surface pattern.

Because of the open structure of the patterns that are created, this type of work is delightful left as it is or backed with a contrasting fabric to create a picture or wall panel. Cutting unevenly, changing the direction of the cut, and cutting with sharp decorative scissors leads to endless creative possibilities. I would strongly recommend that you try out the cut pattern on paper before you do it on the silk paper: cut once measure twice!

Patterns are formed b cutting and folding si sheets. All these pieces have been embellished with beads that secure the folded flaps and enhance the overall shapes.

DECORATIVE FOLDING

This is a lovely way to create a simple book from one sheet of silk paper. It also allows for the addition of many decorative details. The doubled pages can be made into pockets by only sealing two rather than three edges. Apertures can be cut out to enable other flat decorative items to be framed.

Begin by making a large piece of silk paper using the iron method. The size you make will depend on the eventual page size you want. For example, a finished page size of 10 x 10cm (4 x 4 in) requires a minimum sheet size of 40 x 40cm (16 x 16 in) as the starting size; a page measuring 13 x 10cm (5 x 4 in) requires a sheet 50 x 40cm (20 x 16 in).

Following the template (see page 124), mark and cut out a sheet the correct size. Draw fold lines onto the silk with a soft pencil and ruler. Each line should be folded and creased up and down several times (mountain and valley folds) before cutting, to help in the assembly of the book. If you wish, you can make a decorative cover by measuring the size of the pages, adding the width of the spine, and cutting this shape out of silk paper (or indeed any other fabric). You may wish to support it with a lightweight material, such as Vilene. The book can be glued or stitched into position.

Above Use mountain and valley folds to create a simple book out of a piece of silk paper.

Opposite You can glue or sew a decorativ cover onto your book.

Making a book

Highly embellished sheets of silk paper look lovely bound together to make books. Here, I added paper flowers and metallic flakes to silk fibres after they were sprayed with colour and before they were ironed. Ironing makes the extra elements adhere to the surface. The papers were then left to dry. Each paper was further decorated with paint, stitching and embellishments such as tin leaves, ribbons and lace. Once all the surface embellishments had been added, I sandwiched interlining material (cut slightly smaller than the silks) between the papers. I stitched some of these sandwiches together by hand with running stitch or more complicated stitches, such as knotted button hole to create an edge detail.

Don't worry if the sheets are slightly different sizes: this all adds to the creative look of the finished item. Place lace or ribbon loops evenly along the inside edge; these can either be sewn on top or inserted between the layers of the sandwich to give a neater appearance. These are then used to fasten the book pages together.

TIP

If you choose to machine stitch the pages, you need to consider the colour of the top thread and the bottom bobbin as both will be seen. The stitch style is up to you.

Books of silk paper samples allow you to combine favourite decorative techniques

THE MEDIUM METHOD

In the iron method, silk paper is made from fibres that contain the gum sericin, which is activated by heat and moisture. In the medium method, silk that has had the gummy sericin removed is used. This is because the method reintroduces glue to bind the fibres together. Glues that may be used are PVA, marvin medium and acrylic medium, all of which have a variety of finishes. The glue used for the project shown opposite was an acrylic medium with a matt finish, although you can use glue with another finish, such as satin and gloss. Should you wish, these mediums can also be tinted with acrylic colour or metallic flakes. None of the projects in this section had colours added to the medium, which was diluted to approximately one part medium to five parts water (a 1:5 ratio). The strength of the bonding medium should be determined by its final use: if you are making a bag from the silk fabric created, you will need a stronger mix because the bag will be handled. A weaker mix will suffice for a more decorative piece.

Both naturally coloured and dyed silks can be used for this method. If using dyed silks, you may find that there is a small leaching of dye colour into the medium mix. In my experience, this does not affect the outcome of the piece: just be aware that this slight discolouration might happen.

SAFETY:

Wash your hands with hot, soapy water if
you get any kind of medium on your hands.

YOU WILL NEED:

- 2 pieces of lightweight lint-free cloth,
  cut to size
- shallow plastic tray
- dyed silk top or other gum-out fibres
- hot water (just off the boil)
- large spoon
- large bowl or jug for the 1:5
  ratio medium

1 Place the cloth on the bottom of the shallow tray. Pull out fibres from the tops and lay in a north–south direction. The pulls of silk should slightly overlap like roof tiles. Leave a narrow border between the fibres and the edge of the tray.

2 Lay a second layer of silk at right angles to the first layer, again slightly overlapping like roof tiles.

3 Place a second piece of cloth over the silk layers.

4 Pour enough nearly boiling water over the cloth just to wet the fibres. Take care when doing this.

5 Using the back of the spoon, carefully burnish the surface of the fibre sandwich. This process allows you to spread the water evenly, distributing it throughout the fibre layers. You may need to add a little more water, but don't worry if you seem to have too much as you can pour any excess away. Burnishing helps the fibres to connect using any residue of sericin. If you left the silk layers to dry out at this stage they would bind together, but it would be an extremely fragile connection because these fibres have had most of their sericin removed.

6 When the water has cooled, roll up the sandwich of fibres and submerge it into medium mix.

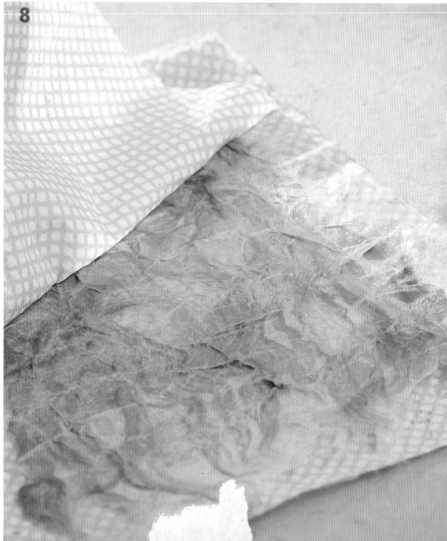

Squash the roll to pump the medium throughout the fibre bundle.

Squeeze out as much of the medium as you can, even out the roll, and open out the fibre sandwich.

At this point, you can leave the piece you have created to dry as it is or fold over the edges as shown here. Whichever you choose to do, cover the fibres again and place the sandwich back into the medium for one final soaking.

0 Squeeze out any excess medium and unwrap. Allow the silk paper to dry before use.

Right The silk rectangle made on pages 70 to 73 with dyed silk tops has a highly textured surface. By placing it on a background of paper made using the iron method, the contrast is enhanced. The spirals were cut from flat, iron method silk paper and attached with a free motion embroidery pattern of freely drawn spirals. A hint of colour was painted on the edge of the spirals so they look as though they are subtly lifting from the surface.

TYPES OF SILK THAT CAN BE USED IN THE MEDIUM METHOD

mulberry (white) tops

tussah (honey-coloured) tops

throwster's waste

condenser waste

split carrier rods

filament

noil variants

Random texture

this example, you can see the effect
using a variety of natural, undyed
res laid out randomly. Highly
xtured surfaces can be created using
is process.

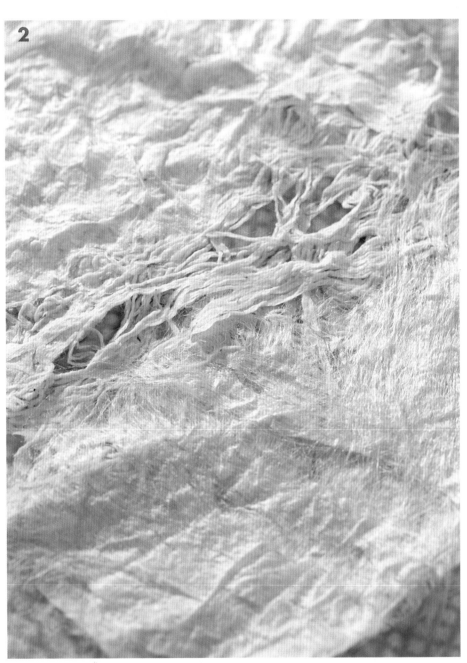

Lay out the silk fibres: these do not
have to be aligned so long as they
overlap and connect. However,
aligning fibres will create a
stronger fabric. Follow Steps 1 to 4
on page 71, omit Step 5, then
continue to the end.

2 By omitting the burnishing step,
the end result will be much more
textured. After scrunching to
remove the excess medium, the
fabric can be left to dry naturally,
in which case the texture will be
very prominent. Alternatively, it
can be gently flattened by hand to
reduce the height of the texture. It
can also be ironed in places to
create a contrast of texture.

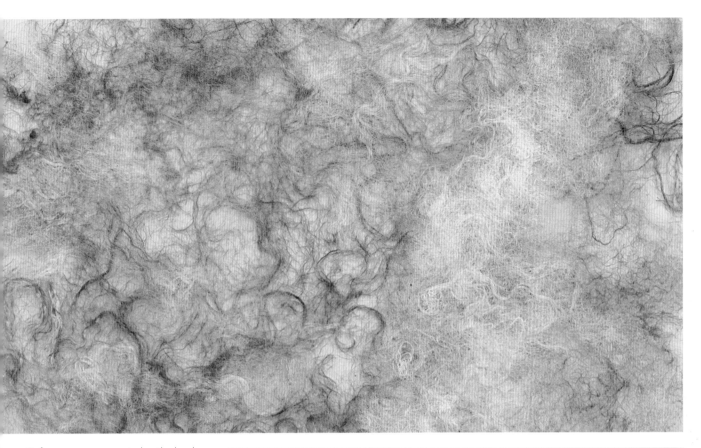

bove Soft textures are created with dyed
owster's waste, resulting in a delicate,
en structure.

ght This image shows fibres contrasting in
th colour and texture.

he textured silk
ackground (made on
age 75) is an ideal
upport for natural
rchin spines. Simple
and stitching with
nen thread
mphasises the
ontrasting textures.

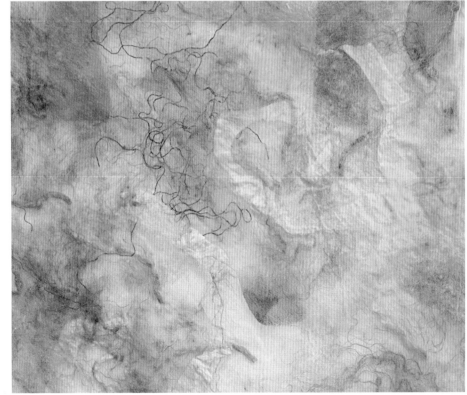

Manipulating fibres

The samples on these pages were made by layering loose silk fibres that had been soaked in a medium onto dyed wet-strength tissue. This tissue is known by various names, including repair tissue and bookbinders' tissue, and has properties that are very useful to textile makers. It absorbs colour and remains very strong when wet, rather like a fine fabric. When dry, it retains the crispness of paper and can be folded neatly. If the surface is scrunched up, rolled and generally softened, it will have the qualities of a draping fabric. It is lightweight and can be stitched and over-coloured.

The technique is a little messy, but very rewarding. Place your chosen fibres directly into a bowl of medium. Wearing rubber or latex gloves, squish and squash the fibres until they are saturated. Remove the fibres from the bowl, squeezing out the excess medium, then open and tease them into shapes. Arrange the fibres on the dyed wet-strength tissue; you can move the fibres around until the medium begins to dry out. When dry, another layer of silk fibres can be added and again allowed to dry thoroughly. Please note that if you make a very deep surface using this method the drying time will be considerable. Layered surfaces can be made to a reasonable height, but layering does take quite a while (several days) and patience!

Dyed silk tops soaked in medium were pulled out into free form organic shapes then laid on a dyed wet-strength tissue background.

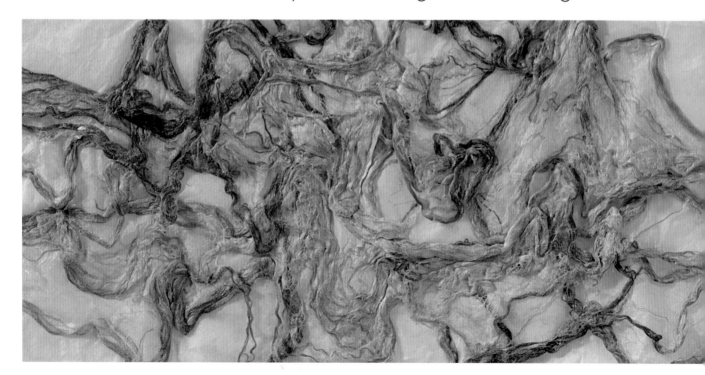

low A combination of dyed throwster's
aste and condenser waste was laid out on
ed wet-strength tissue. This was further
orned with commercially cut, glittered
wer shapes, attached by free machining
to the textured surface. Iridescent glass
wer beads complete the panel.

Here, dyed silk noil was soaked and laid out
on dyed wet-strength tissue before being
embellished with stitch method flowers with
antique button beads in their centres.

Casting with a block

Casting on a block is messier than the embossing method shown on page 50, but it is fun and the results are worthwhile. In the iron method, gummy fibres are used, which results in a smooth surface to the embossed paper. In this casting method, non-gummy fibres soaked in a medium are employed, which gives the paper far more texture.

The process is a variation on the medium method and works most efficiently with short-fibered silks such as noils. You may wish to try casting with other fibres, but the results will vary.

Wearing rubber or latex gloves, plunge the noil fibres into a concentrated medium. Squish and squash them until they are saturated,

then lift the fibres and squeeze out the excess medium. Open out the noil fibre mass and spread it into thin layers on top of a deeply etched moulding block. Press the fibres into the mould. If holes appear in the silk layer, either add more saturated fibres or just accept the holes and see them as a creative bonus.

Turn over the moulding block onto a plastic-covered surface and press down to compact and consolidate the silk cast. Remove the cast by teasing it away from the moulding block and lay the silk cast aside to dry. At this stage you can create a 3-D piece. Place the cast over a suitable object, such as a plastic cup, and when the cast is dry it will take the shape of that object. To make a flat piece, lay out the cast silk on a flat surface.

Left In this sample, I enhanced the casts with a fine layer of acrylic paint and used small flowers to attach them to a fabric background. Each flower was stitched through with a sequin and a bead.

It is important to remove the silk cast immediately from the moulding block, as it will adhere if allowed to dry. When dry, the silk cast can be painted or enhanced with patinating waxes. The cast pieces can be used as art works in their own right or cut out and attached to other textile surfaces with glue or stitches.

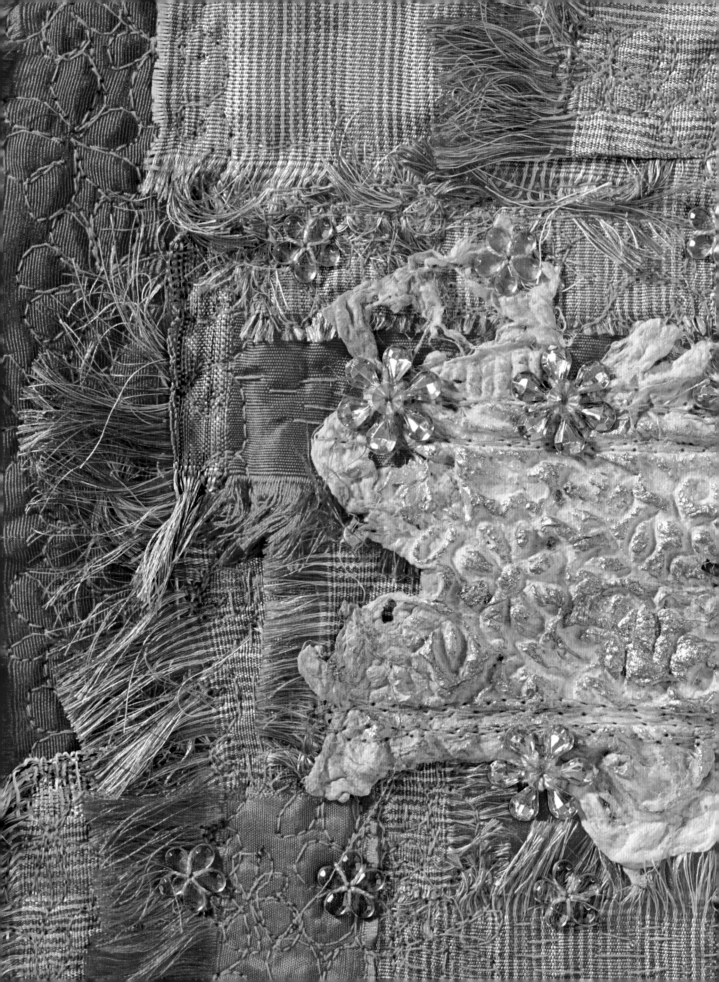

NOIL FIBRES

The samples on pages 80 to 83 were made with noil. There are two kinds: tussah noil is a golden coloured fibre that can be natural or dyed; clean, bleached noil is a whiter fibre that is also available in natural or dyed form. See page 126 for more on noil.

Creating texture with an iron

A wide selection of silk types is used in this method of making a textured surface. The larger the 'palette' of silks you have, the greater the decorative possibilities. Although the effect is seen more easily using natural tones, such as the ones used here, combinations of coloured and natural fibres or coloured fibres only can be used.

Make a sheet of silk paper using the medium method and leave to dry. Cover the areas to be ironed with a piece of silicone or greaseproof paper and, with the iron on the hottest setting, press down and smooth over the area you want to 'shine'. This takes only a moment so don't linger on any area. Small travel irons are best as they have a smaller area than ordinary domestic irons. Hoof irons or quilting irons are even smaller, making them useful for this process. Papers treated to smoothing can be further embellished with matt and shiny threads.

This technique can be used to create considerable contrast or more subtle and elegant pieces. If you use mulberry and tussah tops, you will notice that the ironed areas will really shine and shimmer in contrast to areas that are left un-ironed. Areas on your design that have shorter more textured silk areas will be smoothed and offer a contrast of texture.

TYPES OF SILK THAT CAN BE USED

tussah (honey-coloured) tops

mulberry (white) tops

noil variants

previously made silk papers

Making bowls

I decided to use cellulose paste as the medium for this project. Many people like to use cellulose paste to make bowls because it is easier to apply than liquid medium. It also allows you to make a stiffer vessel that will stand more easily. Cellulose paste without fungicide is widely available from DIY and craft stores. Choose paste that is intended for super-durable anaglypta or heavy embossed papers. For a bowl you only need about a pint of liquid, so do not make up the full amount in the packet. If you choose to use an acrylic medium instead, make a strong mixture and be prepared for a little difficulty when removing the cast from the clingfilm.

YOU WILL NEED:

- large bowl or jug for the paste
- cling film
- an object to mould around
- brown paper
- cellulose paste or medium (1 tbs to 300ml/½ pint) of cold water)
- paintbrush
- dyed hankies
- ruler
- black marker pen
- latex or rubber gloves
- scissors

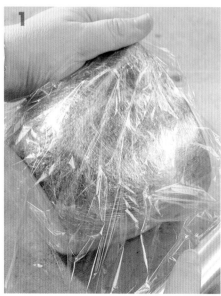

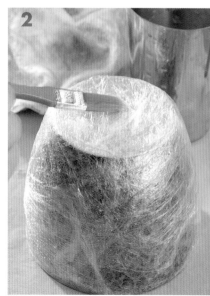

Cover your chosen mould with generous layers of good quality cling film.

Protect your work surface with brown paper. Separate out two or three layers of dyed hankies. Using the cellulose paste, paste the covered surface of the wrapped mould.

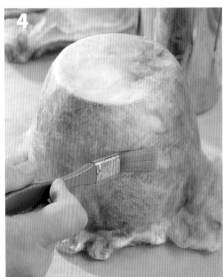

Place a stretched silk hankie over the mould. Pull it down to cover the mould.

When the hankie is fully stretched over the mould, reapply a generous layer of cellulose paste over the entire surface. You will notice that the silk becomes translucent as the cellulose paste soaks in.

Continue adding layers of stretched silk hankies over the mould, covering each layer with plenty of cellulose paste. You should repeat at least three to four times. If you require a very substantial bowl, I would recommend using six to eight hankies. A delicate bowl with a translucent effect would only require two to four layers.

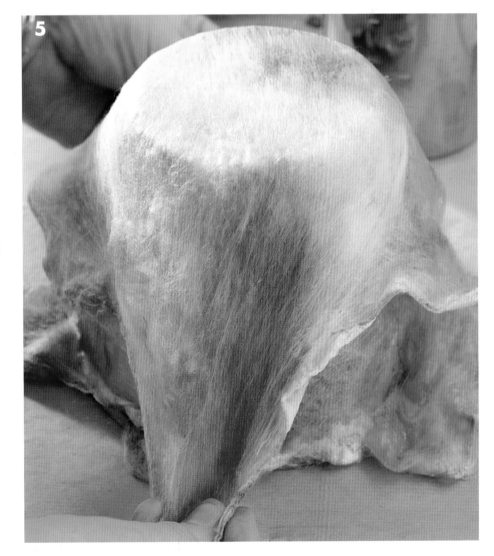

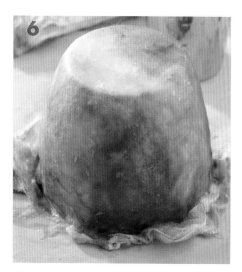

6 When you are happy with the thickness of the bowl, cover with a final layer of glue.

7 Apply glue until there are no dry patches left. Do not worry about the dry bottom edge: this will be cut off after the silk cast has dried. The completed cast should be left to dry in a warm environment. Depending on how many layers and the ambient temperature of the drying place, this can take one or more days.

8 When the silk cast is completely dry, gently ease the shape off the mould. Slip a flat knife in between the cling film and the silk cast and run the blade around the mould or, if you are brave, simply peel the cast away. The cast is easily reshaped and generally returns to its original state.

TIP

Choose a mould that will allow for easy removal the cast. If you choose a mould with an intricate shape, the cast can be cut down in order to remove it and then re-pasted to create a whole shape. This is quite difficult to achieve so, until yo have gained experience in this method, I would strongly recommend the use of a gently tapering mould, such as a vase or a small basin.

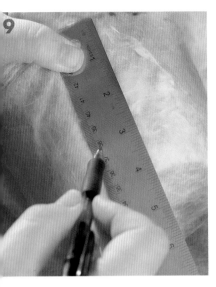

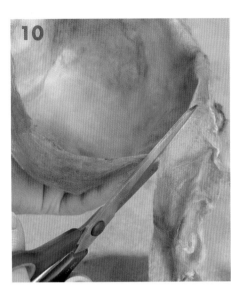

9 With a ruler and a pen, measure and mark a line along the top where you want to remove the excess from the cast.

10 Using a sharp pair of long-bladed scissors, cut decisively along the marked line. If small-bladed scissors are used, a smooth cut line will be difficult to achieve.

11 At this stage, you can add a small amount of sealant (either more cellulose paste or acrylic medium, depending on what you used) or some acrylic paint to the cut edge to seal it. Alternatively, it can be left as it is. I finished the edge of the bowl with individual leaves made using the stitched method, described on page 94. The veins of each leaf were defined with machine stitches before each piece was stitched on by hand.

Left This vessel was moulded around a jam jar. The rim clearly shows the natural ripple of the edges of the mawata hankies from which the bowl was made. The body of the bowl has been enhanced with an undulating machine-stitched line that complements the ripple of the edge.

Opposite The edge of this delicate bowl was cut away to neaten it, then decorated with machine zigzag stitch and beads.

THE STITCHED METHOD

A beautiful fabric can be created from silk fibres by using free-machine embroidery combined with water-soluble film. Pre-programmed or free-machine embroidery allows a delicate filigree of loose silk fibres to be connected, whatever their form. Free-machine embroidery requires three changes to the set up of your machine. Refer to your manual when changing settings, as each machine has its own set up parameters. Many people feel that they can use a bare needle. This is dangerous as a moment's distraction can cause injury and machines are designed to form the stitch properly when a foot is attached.

The type of water-soluble film used in this method is a self-supporting film that requires no further stabilisation. This means that you should not need a frame to control the movement of the silk sandwich as you work. The film is generally sold under the trade name Romeo, but is available under other names and is designed to work in a wide range of climate conditions. It is a heavyweight transparent film that remains inert until soaked in water. It does not have a top surface and either side can be used. Some films have a sticky feel in very humid climatic conditions but this should not affect their function. Check with your local craft suppliers and always read the manufacturer's instructions if in doubt.

THE STITCHED METHOD

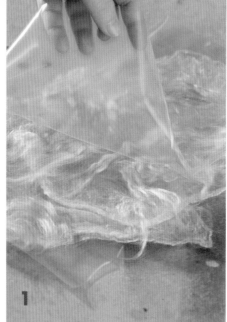

SAFETY:

The feed dog must be lowered or covered and it is essential that the appropriate free-motion foot is attached. It is very dangerous to sew without a foot attached and the stitches will be formed incorrectly.

YOU WILL NEED:

- 1 sheet of Romeo water-soluble material or equivalent film
- dyed hankie
- dyed silk tops
- sewing machine
- threads – cotton, synthetic or silk
- black marker pen
- ruler
- scissors

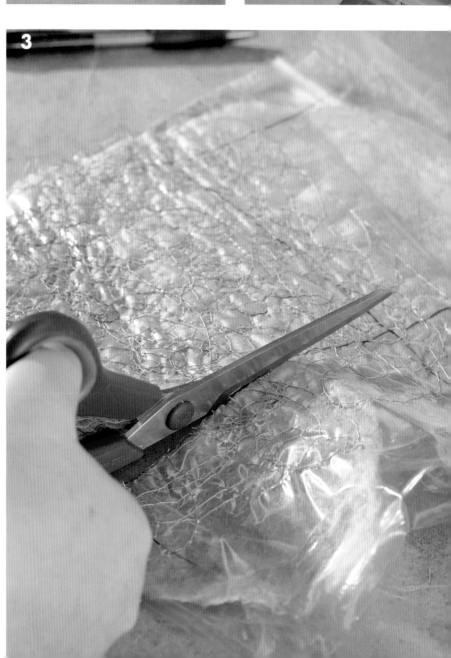

Most water-soluble films are folded over so first need to be opened up. If you have a product that is a single sheet, you will need two pieces about the same size. Select your silk fibres. I chose a dyed hankie split into quite thin layers and silk tops in a contrasting colour. Don't worry about over-lapping the hankies, as it makes little difference to the thickness of the layers. Fold over the top layer of water-soluble film to make a silk sandwich.

Set your machine to free machine mode – no feed dogs, no stitch length or stitch width. Sew across the silk sandwich in a gentle looping motion to create an interlocking structure.

With a marker pen, draw out a square 15 x 15 cm (6 x 6 in) and cut out.

Keep the off-cuts for use in another project.

TIP

You can use a different colour thread or, indeed, thickness of thread on the bottom bobbin to that of the top thread, as your work may be seen from both sides.

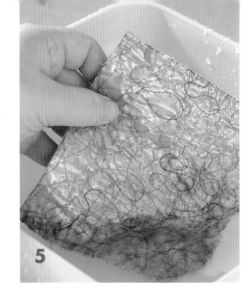

5 Place the newly created fabric into a bowl of warm water and allow it to soak for about twenty minutes. It is at this stage that the water-soluble film will dissolve and dissipate from the fabric into the water. You may need to repeat this process to remove all the water-soluble film. The film will become gelatinous and dissolve in the water, which will go cloudy.

6 Allow the silk square to dry out on a paper towel. If you wish, you can iron the dried fabric flat or leave it un-ironed for an interesting, irregular texture.

Right I transformed the silk paper square into this dainty container by cutting a second square of silk fabric the same size as the first, folding over the corners and then sewing the edges together to create a container. I overlaid tight satin stitches and looser zigzag stitches to create an interesting effect. Finally, I edged the corner triangles with beads.

To create this tiara, I placed a combination of dyed silk hankies and silk tops between two sheets of water-soluble film. After drawing on the outline of a tiara, I filled in the shape with matching thread, using free motion embroidery. When the film had dissolved, I sewed the stitched piece onto a lightweight Vilene backing and embellished it with twinkling gems and gold beads

Making a scarf

Creating larger items, such these scarves, requires a little more preparation than for a small piece made from the stitch method. When laying out the fibres, give some thought to the colour, texture and shape of the final item. You may wish to use various silk fibres in a single colour throughout or use two colours: one on the bottom layer and one on the top so that the scarf will be a different colour on each side. Colour could also flow from one end to the other randomly or be laid out in a controlled, graduated manner.

A long slim scarf with rounded ends is a simple shape to start with, but you can choose more innovative shapes. Cut out wavy or curled shapes from spare fabric to see how the finished scarf will drape or fall around your neck. Use this as your template. The length is dependent on personal preference: measure a favourite scarf to get an idea of the length you need. Using different threads on the top and bottom bobbin will create colour variation. You should also consider the stitch you are going to use. A dense stitch pattern will create a stiffer result than an open, lace-like stitch pattern, which will give the finished scarf a more fluid drape.

Draw around the template onto water-soluble fabric with a marker pen. Remove the template and save it for future projects. Hand tack around the edges to secure the layers together with large bold stitches. Alternatively, there are temporary adhesives (especially created for textile artists) that dissolve with the water-soluble film. When the layers are complete and secure, roll up the sandwich so that you have about 20cm (8 in) available to stitch on. Stitch this area, then open up the roll to expose more unstitched area. As you progress, the stitched area can be rolled up to make it easier to manipulate.

When the body of the scarf has been fully stitched, open out the roll and consider the edges. A simple zigzag satin stitch sewn around the perimeter the scarf is a simple way to bind the edges or create a selvedge. Make a sample to test the effect before starting on the scarf edges. (If the edge stitchi is too tight or dense, this will affect the drape of the scarf.) When the stitching is complete, dissolve the water-soluble film as described on page 98 and leave to dry.

The addition of beads and stitched dangles or indeed any embellishment will personalise your piece. Adding beads to the ends of your scarf will he it hang better when worn.

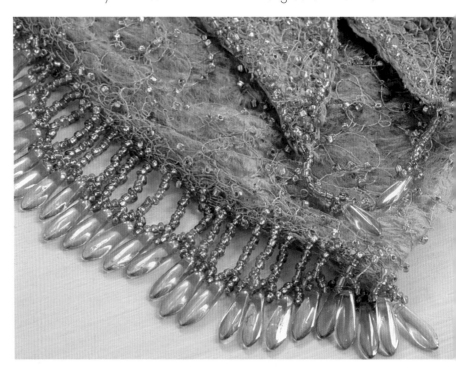

Making jewellery

Small pieces of silk paper made using the stitched method can be further embellished and transformed into exciting pieces of jewellery. To create these necklaces, make up as many stitched shapes as you desire for your necklace. Trace around the templates (see page 124) onto water-soluble film and stitch within the shapes. Make the units in pairs (back and front) or folded.

Rows of concentric stitching on the circular shapes will makes the final pieces slightly elastic and so make padding them easier. On larger circles concentric stitching works equally well, but small overlapping squiggles give a more organic effect. Cut light-weight craft felt or other appropriate material just smaller than the unit and use several layers, each smaller than the other, to give a domed effect to the jewellery. Stitch the units together by hand using appropriately coloured thread. Use a ladder stitch to create a firm edge; if a slip stitch is used to bind over the edge, the result will be softer. A machine zigzag stitch can be used, but mind your fingers because the pieces will be quite small. The completed units can be stitched together with beads or by laying cording between the elements as you stitch. Enhance the units with seed beads or other decorative elements.

TIP

The combination of colour, texture and stitch marks is very important for these small jewellery items: all the elements should work well together to create a harmonious ensemble for you to wear.

Using pre-programmed stitches

Take a good look at your sewing machine manual to familiarise yourself with the many ways that the machine can be pre-programmed to create stitch patterns. Don't be put off if you have an older or a more basic machine: utilitarian stitches, such as blind hemming, zigzag and buttonhole can be used in a very creative and decorative manner. Unique surfaces can be achieved by sewing stitches very close together, by overlaying them or by using a variety of shiny metallic or variegated threads.

The easy way to use pre-programmed stitches to create a piece of silk paper is to choose the default pattern that the machine uses without human intervention. Before stitching onto silk fibres, carry out a test on a trial cloth: by altering the stitch width and length many variations can be achieved. Remember that the purpose behind the stitching is to connect the silk fibres between the interlocking stitches. Follow the instructions for the stitched method on pages 96 to 98.

To make a handy evening bag, create a number of squares using pre-programmed stitches, with zigzag stitches around the edges to form individual units. A bag can then be constructed by linking these squares together (see template page 124). Hand stitching is a lovely final adornment to the surface.

TIP

It is always a good idea to read your sewing machine manual every now and again. I nearly always discover something that I had forgotten and find inspiration in revisiting the more simple stitch patterns.

This evening bag was made out of seventeen squares, each of which was embellished with different pre-programmed stitches. When the squares were completed, I removed the water-soluble film and hand stitched the bag together.

Making a stitched vessel

This vessel may look complex, but it is actually constructed from a rectangle and a circle then manipulated into a more free-form shape by tucking and pleating. You will need a dyed silk cap, some dyed throwster and a compass or circular object to draw around in addition to the materials listed on page 96. If you want to create a delicate vessel, use thin layers of silk cap. If you require a more robust or solid structure, add more layers of silk at the stage of assembling the silk sandwich.

Stretch a silk cap and lay it out on a sheet of water-soluble film, filling in any thin areas. (Regardless of the density of the fabric you want to create, even layers are better than uneven layers.) Distribute some throwster's waste over the cap to add drama to the surface. Fold over the water-soluble film and draw a rectangle and circle on it with a marker pen. Outline the edges of these shapes with a free motion straight stitch. This will give you a stronger, more resilient edge that will provide a consistent and non-distorting shape when the vessel is assembled. Stitch the rectangle and circle in free motion stitc pattern of your choice.

When the pieces are completely stitched, cut them out and leave a tiny margin to the edge of the stitch lines. Using a zigzag or satin stitch to bind the stitches over will strengthen and fo a selvedge to make the construction easier. Dissolve the water-soluble film and leave the shapes to dry. When, d iron them flat then assemble the vessel with a machine stitch or by hand. To create the freeform shape, make a tuc and use a running stitch to secure it.

TIP

If you want to line your vessel, copy the original template but allow an extra margin a around. Assemble and use a small catch or slip edge to secure the lining to the inner edge of the vessel. If you decide not to line it, use variegated thread on the bobbin sc when the vessel is made up, there will be a quirky colour mix visible on the inside. Alternatively, use a contrasting colour to add drama to the piece.

Hydrangea panels

An artistic combination of silk paper methods was employed to create these pieces. I began by printing onto pieces of iron method silk paper with a stamp made from compacted polystyrene packaging cut into a small rectangle and glued to a cardboard backing. The image was incised into the surface of the polystyrene with a stylus. A more permanent block can be made from lino or printers' rubber, but this will take longer to create. The stamped pieces were set aside.

I loosely stitched together some dyed silk fibres following the stitched method. I then cut up the stitched sheet and rewove the strips before adding free-machine stitches over the new structure. This was then soaked to remove the water-soluble film, left to dry, then set aside.

Another key element in these panels is iron method paper (pages 32 to 67) with naturally dried out hydrangea flowers incorporated into it. Once the various elements had been assembled, it was time to arrange them and stitch them together. In a collage like this, the balance of the piece should be borne mind. Use paper pieces to practice yo arrangement before you commit to sewing down the silk elements. My hydrangea panels were further adorne with more free-machine stitching across the surface. Free-machine flowers and patched slips (a slip is a separate element added to the main piece) wer dotted around the surface to create a harmonious composition.

Strips of stitched method silk fabric were woven together and restitched before the water-soluble stabiliser was removed.

Left Detail of free-machine hydrangea flowers made from sheer fabric.

TIP

If you want to create an iron method paper with petal inclusions, choose a flower that is not too fleshy. When these flowers are dried out, they may not give a wholly satisfactory result. Flowers such as roses (petals only) lobelia, pansies and violets dry well and still retain some colour.

WEAVING AND OVERDYEING RODS

This chapter demonstrates some of the ways in which rods and cocoons can be used to create decorative pieces with a strong structural element by cutting, slicing, overdyeing, inserting and painting them. Working with these rigid structures is very different to working with the fibres used in previous chapters. Using rods and cocoons, both whole and cut, allows the structural character to remain, even when stretched and (in the case of rods) twisted. As the photograph opposite shows, dyed and stretched rods make an attractive panel. Cocoons particularly come into their own when used for jewellery, giving an ageless elegance and durability to any design.

Weaving and overdyeing

hen you separate layers from dyed
ds, the areas of dye penetration will
revealed. If you discover areas that
undyed, there are several options
ailable to you: one is to accept and
nbrace these undyed areas within
ur work! Alternatively, you can go
er the undyed areas with textile paint,
mply letting the paint dry (if the piece
ll be used for decorative purposes
ly) or fixing it by following the
anufacturer's instructions. My favourite
pproach is to paint the undyed areas

with acid dyes, using a sponge brush
(see page 24) to spot colour certain
areas or by total immersion. Rather nice
colour combinations can be achieved
by overdyeing the rod slivers completely.

In this sample, I created a woven
background using rods and decorative
elements that were edged with machine
stitching. The piece shows the subtlety of
colour that can be achieved by dyeing
then overdyeing rods. I separated
selected rods then wove them together
to form a sheet of silk. I supported the

loosely woven structure by placing it on
a lightweight Vilene backing. This
allowed me to control the structure and
stitch over the surface more efficiently. I
added stitched elements to the surface
to reinforce the block-and-line surface of
the silk panel background. You may
wish to cut the rod layers along their
length and weave them over the rest to
create a more intricate woven fabric.
Leave the joins exposed or hide them
under the woven layers, as you prefer.

MAKING A COLLAGE

Woven silk paper panels don't have to be complex. Here, rods were laid out to show the colours to best effect. The delicate panel was created by using machine stitches to trap split dyed rods. These were first laid out in a carefully graduated way to form a subtle flow of colour. When I was happy with the arrangement, I stitched the rods onto a lightweight Vilene background.

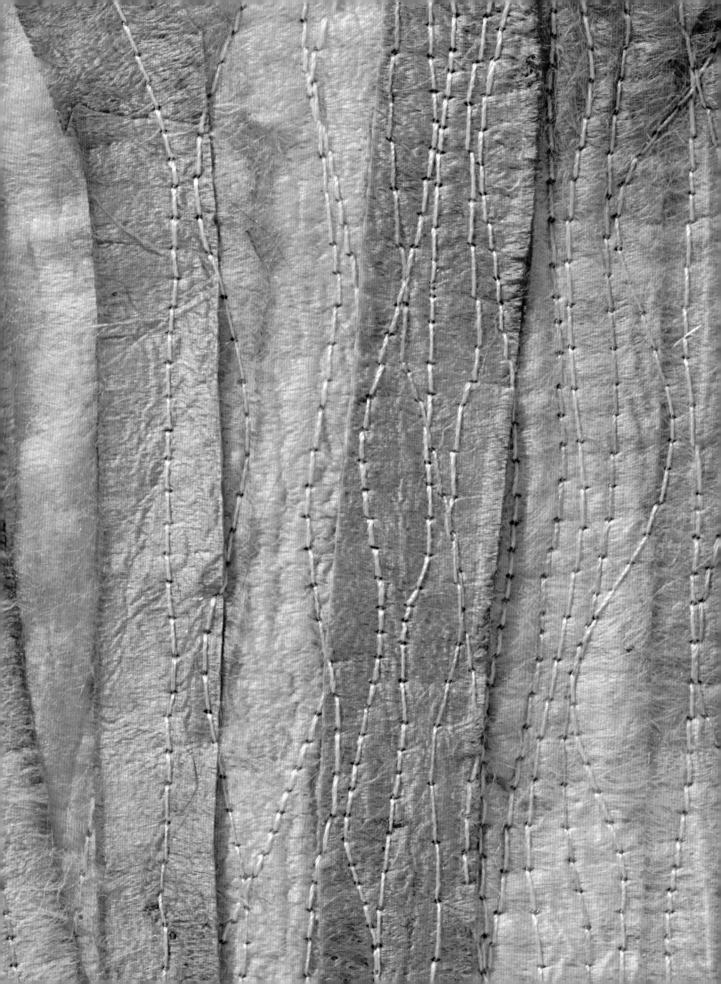

Creating roses

To create these charming flowers, select at least three rods for each rose you wish to create. Process each rod to give you a number of layers following the method shown on page 14. From these separated layers, select those whose colour is most appropriate for the centres (the bud) and those that are more suited for the faded petals of the outside of the rose. Curl back each layer so that the heart of the rose has an outward curve. Stitch the rose together at the base of the bud then attach the outer petals. You will find that each layer from a rod will stretch quite considerably and may even start to twist naturally on itself to form a rosette with barely any effort on your part. Stitch the stretched-out layer to the base of the bud, adding more layers until the flow is to your liking. A large, dramatic tea rose can be achieved by attaching the bud and basic rose shape to a fabric backing, then stitching more rods to th background to create a larger flower head.

TIP

For a more natural effect, the rods can be dyed to rose-like colours. The 'roses' can be enhanced further by inserting fringes in between the layers as they are made, and you can create 'dew' by adding a drop or two of a clear-drying glue to the edges.

Making vessels

ese decorative containers are made
m overdyed silk rods that were first
lit and laid onto a lightweight Vilene
cking. I used free-machine
broidery to attach the rod slivers to
e backing to create a sheet of fabric.
m this I cut four rectangles
proximately 7.5 x 18cm (3 x 7 in)
d a base piece 8cm (3 in) square.
ned each of these pieces, attaching
e lining by using a zigzag stitch
ound the edges. Finally, I assembled
e containers with hand stitches and
ged the joins with beads.

Cocoon jewellery

On pages 12 to 13, I demonstrated how cocoons could be processed by soaking and stretching. However, cocoons can be used whole or cut with scissors or a sharp craft knife. Whole cocoons are usually quite even in size and small bells can be made by varying the angle and the position of the cut. These bells can then be painted with various media to create exceptionally decorative units. Alternatively, you may wish to use pre-dyed cocoons. Adding beads will result in an even more luxurious effect, but I strongly advise using a thimble to sew through what is a very dense material. I used cotton threads for all these jewellery projects, but this is a purely personal preference for natural materials. The use of synthetic or metallic threads can add a delightful layer of decoration. In this piece, the bells were painted in contrasting colours then beads were stitched around the bell openings. The bells were then stitched onto a cord.

TIP

The most efficient way to pierce the dense surface of a cocoon is to pierce the cocoo first with a stiletto (a hard steel point) or a crafter's piercing tool. Alternatively, use a finely gauged needle such as a size 10 milliner's needle. This type of strong piercing needle allows small beads to be threaded over the eye.

LAYERING COCOONS

A simple but very decorative neck piece can be made by threading beaded stalks onto a cord and adding bells to the ends of the cords. I began by selecting several pairs of cut cocoons, making sure one of each pair would fit inside the other. The cocoons were then coloured with acid dyes rather than painted and the larger cocoons were cut into five or six petals, which were then carefully cut into more rounded shapes. The dyed petal-shaped cases were then slipped over the smaller cocoons and decorated with hand stitching. I made small tassels out of multicoloured threads and glued them in position, although they could be stitched. These units were then threaded onto a beaded stalk and attached to a cord that was finished with metal clam shells.

Decorative panels

Whether dyed or natural, split cocoons
arranged on a sympathetic background
make unusual panels that look great
framed and hung on a wall or
displayed flat on a table. In the orange
sample (opposite), dyed whole cocoons
were cut in half, arranged in rows – cut
side down – and stitched down onto a
fabric background to create a striking
decorative panel. Blue beads were
chosen to accent the bright orange dye.

Right Silk paper made using the medium
method was cut, stitched and decorated with
half cocoons and buttons.

Left This decorative panel uses laterally sliced, whole cocoons which have been placed inside each other and stitched dow The silk paper background is detailed furth with mother-of-pearl discs and sheer yarn-thread stitchery.

Top left (opposite) Here, dyed, cut cocoon were stitched with contrasting thread to create organic form.

Top right (opposite) Sliced, cut cocoons together with variegated thread create a limpet-like surface.

Bottom right (opposite) In this example, whole cocoons were sliced laterally and painted with metallic textile paint on the outside and metal flake on the inside. They were then connected with linen cord and threaded with beads for detailing.

Bottom left (opposite) Whole cocoons and smaller cut cocoons were sliced and place inside each other to create delicate porcelain-like structures.

Templates

Enlarge the templates to suit your designs. Copy the Hydrangea and Necklace templates onto cardstock, lay the templates onto silk paper and draw around the shapes with a fine pencil. Draw the Booklet pattern directly onto a sheet of silk paper using a soft pencil and ruler. The Evening Bag pattern shows how seventeen silk paper square can be sewn together and folded to create a purse.

p.42, Hydrangea
Fold all petals along the fold lines, crease and unfold. Fold one petal in again. Rotate the flower clockwise and fold the next petal in. As you fold the third petal, gently lift the lobe of the first petal to allow the third to slip underneath. Fold the fourth petal, again lifting the first petal to interlock all four petals.

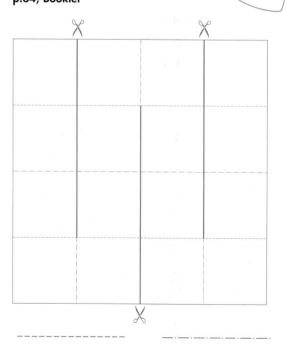

p.64, Booklet

Key for valley fold   **Key for mountain fold**

p.102-103, Necklaces
Follow the instructions on page 102 to make up the two necklaces. The diamond and large circle are folded in half and padded, whereas the small circle is doubled up and padded.

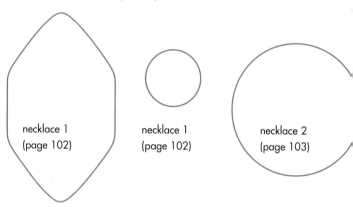

necklace 1
(page 102)

necklace 1
(page 102)

necklace 2
(page 103)

p.104, Evening Bag
Sew side A to A, B to B, etc., leaving the short outer edges unsewn. Fold up a rectangle in the center to form the base of the bag.

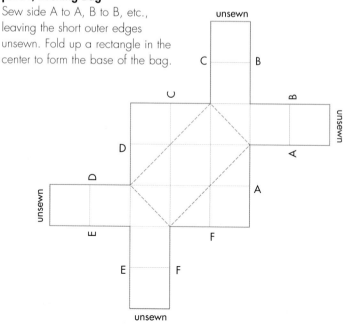

unsewn

C   B

unsewn

D

A

unsewn

E   F

E   F

unsewn

Suppliers

lk fibres are not available from eneral craft stores, but there are a umber of companies worldwide who pply them. All the suppliers listed here re knowledgeable, carry a wide ariety of silk fibre and related products nd will despatch fibres to customers.

anvas

nnégatan 57

13 08 GÖTEBORG

weden

ww.canvasshop.se

arries a wide range of dyed and ndyed silk fibres as well as many other ems used within the book.

raftynotions Ltd.

nit 2 Jessop Way

ewark NG24 2ER

nited Kingdom

ww.craftynotions.com

Craftynotions is owned and run by Sarah Lawrence and ships worldwide. The company stocks all the products used in this book. Creative Colour Sprays are a Craftynotions brand product but similar products are available from other sources.

Joggles.com, LLC

1454 Main Street Unit 30

West Warwick, RI

USA

www.joggles.com

Supplier of dyed and undyed silk fibres

Rainbow Silks

6 Wheelers Yard,

Great Missenden HP16 0AL

United Kingdom

www.rainbowsilks.co.uk

Supplies dyed and undyed silk fibres

The Silk Route

Cross Cottage,

Cross Lane

Frimley Green

GU16 6LN, UK

www.thesilkroute.co.uk

Specialist in silk threads and fabrics

The Thread Studio

6 Smith Street

Perth

Western Australia

www.thethreadstudio.com

Stocks a wide range of dyed and undyed silk fibres and related materials.

Treenway Silks

501 Musgrave Road

Salt Spring Island

British Columbia, V8K 1V5

Canada

www.treenwaysilks.com

Stocks dyed and undyed silk fibres

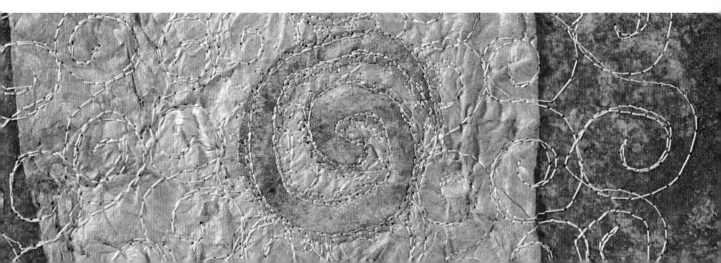

Glossary

BELL

A bell is formed from many silk caps stretched over a single form. A bell may contain up to 1,500 stretched cocoons.

BOMBYX MORI

The silk moth that feeds on mulberry leaves and produces a fine, lustrous filament.

CARDING

The process of combing fibres into alignment.

CARRIER ROD

Guide bar over which the silk is drawn in the process of reeling the silk. Waste silk builds up on this bar and is periodically removed by slitting.

COCOON

A silk cocoon is the result of the process undertaken by the silk worm to create a protective environment while it pupates from a larva to a moth.

COCOON STRIPPINGS

Silk waste from the outer layers of the cocoon which still contains the sericin.

CONDENSER WASTE

Silk condenser waste looks like unspun yarn. The fibres are easily separated.

DEGUMMING

The process of removing the sericin from the silk fibre.

DUPION

A fabric woven from conjoined cocoons.

FIBRION

The inert protein fibre created by silk worms, which is covered with sericin.

FILAMENT

An individual strand of silk which may

Hankie

vary in length from around 450 yards a remarkable 2,000 yards.

HANKIE

Cocoon that has been softened and stretched to form a square shape simila in size to a lady's handkerchief.

MAWATA CAPS

Softened cocoons that are stretched over a bell-shaped form (see Bell).

Carrier rods

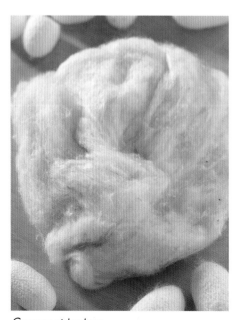

Cocoon strippings

Mawata caps

ULBERRY

ers to the white or common mulberry
sh (*Morus alba*), a small deciduous
e native to China, which is the sole
od of the *Bombyx mori* silk worm.
nce, mulberry silk.

OIL

ort fibres that are created when
oducing a spun silk fibre. Noil fibres
e very light and come in a bulky
rous mass.

AW SILK

k that has been taken from the cocoon
still has the sericin remaining.

ERICIN

e gum surrounding the fibrion fibre,
ich hardens on contact with air,
owing the silk worm to produce its
coon.

Tussah silk noil (top) and clean silk noil

SILK

The product secreted by spinerettes
located on the head of the silk worm.
This hardens on contact with air and is
composed of fibrion and sericin.

SILK SLIVER

Lengths of sliver are thinner than silk tops
and only slightly twisted.

SILK TOP

Broken fibres produced by the cleaning
and carding processes. The fibres
remain aligned to form a continuous
sliver typically used in the spinning
process.

THROWING

The process of creating a silk thread
from filament by winding, doubling
and twisting.

THROWSTER'S WASTE

Residue from the process of "throwing,"
which is the formation of silk thread.

TUSSAH SILK

Silk from worms that are not *Bombyx
mori* and therefore not fed on mulberry.
Tussah is found in many colours from
honey to deep caramel. It tends to be
less lustrous than mulberry silk.

k

*Gummy throwster's waste (top) and
degummed throwster's waste*

*Tussah silk sliver (top) and mulberry silk
sliver*

Index

As many materials and techniques are used throughout the book, the page references are intended to direct the reader to substantial entries only. Page numbers in *italics* refer to illustrations.

AUTHOR'S ACKNOWLEDGEMEN

I would like to thank Fran Lawrence for her nimble ty fingers and tolerance of a aged mother; the team at craftynotions.com and my Christine. Thanks also to Jo Breslich & Foss (and her dc Houdi) for her help, guidar and—above all—patience